COMPILED BY

ALICE GRAY STEVE STEPHENS JOHN VAN DIEST

Multnomah Publishers® *Sisters, Oregon*

# CONTENTS

# NEVER UNDERESTIMATE THE POWER OF LISTS

IF YOU...

- *Scan it*
- *Study it*
- *Ponder it*
- *Discuss it*
- *Share it*
- *Enjoy it*
- *Experience it...*

*A list can change your life!*

Have you ever wondered how some people achieve incredible fulfillment? The answers are in these pages. We've searched the entire universe (well, almost) for the best information—meaningful lists that will move you to action, touch your heart, and change your priorities.

Packed into this third collection of *Lists to Live By* is an abundance of bite-size wisdom for everything that really matters: steps to success, secrets of contentment, fulfillment in marriage, encouragement for tough times, tips for better parenting, enjoyment of life, help for managing finances, and treasures of wisdom and faith.

Never underestimate the power of lists. The *Lists to Live By* books aren't just about things to do; they're about how to be. The information on a single page can inspire, uplift, and chart a new course for your life.

One person summed it up this way:

*Read it, use it, share it, live by it...you'll be surprised at what happens!*

ALICE GRAY    STEVE STEPHENS    JOHN VAN DIEST

# SUCCESS

*Making the most of your life*

1

# TRAITS OF A SUCCESSFUL PERSON

Consciousness of an honest purpose of life.

A just estimate of oneself and everyone else.

Frequent self-examinations.

Steady obedience to what one knows to be right.

Indifference to what others may think or say.

MARCUS AURELIUS
ROMAN EMPEROR

# 10 ACTIONS FOR STAYING MOTIVATED

1. Wake up happy.
2. Use positive self-talk from morning to bedtime.
3. Look at problems as opportunities.
4. Concentrate your energy and intensity without distraction on the successful completion of your current, most important project.
5. Find something good in all your personal relationships and accentuate the blessings.
6. Learn to stay relaxed and friendly no matter how much tension you're under.
7. Think and speak well of your health.
8. Expect the best from others, too.
9. This week, seek out and talk to someone currently doing what you want to do most and doing it well.
10. Remain optimistic by associating with optimists.

DENIS WAITLEY
FROM "THE WINNER'S EDGE"

# NINE INSIGHTS FOR GETTING AHEAD

1. WORK HARD
*Follow tasks through to completion.*

2. THINK CREATIVELY
*See challenges from new angles.*

3. SPEAK GENTLY
*Consider the impact of your words.*

4. COOPERATE FREELY
*Meet the need of the moment—even when it's not yours.*

5. ACT WITH INTEGRITY
*Be the same privately as you are publicly.*

6. HONOR OTHERS
*Recognize your coworkers' contributions.*

7. SEE INSIGHTFULLY
*Look beyond the obvious.*

8. LISTEN THOROUGHLY
*Discern what is meant—not just what is said.*

9. RESPOND APPROPRIATELY
*Deal with mistakes openly and fairly.*

FROM "INSIGHTS NEWSLETTER"
INSIGHT FOR LIVING

# HOW TO LISTEN SO PEOPLE WILL TALK

LOOK AT PEOPLE WHEN THEY SPEAK TO YOU.
*If your eyes are focused elsewhere,*
*it will appear that your mind is as well.*

LEAN FORWARD AS YOU LISTEN.
*Being on the "edge of your seat"*
*shows that, more than just being kind,*
*you are very interested in what they are saying.*

GIVE FEEDBACK.
*Respond by nodding and smiling. Ask questions.*
*This lets the other person know that you were*
*listening closely to what was said.*

DON'T INTERRUPT OR CHANGE THE SUBJECT.
*Let speakers finish their own sentences,*
*and allow them to finish talking about the subject*
*they're discussing, even if it's not your favorite.*

REPEAT BACK TO THEM SOME OF THE THINGS THEY SAID.
*This shows that you were listening.*
*It is also validating and confirming.*

COMPLIMENT THEM ON THEIR INSIGHTS AND WISDOM.
*This will encourage them to continue*
*sharing with you in the future.*

SHOW YOUR APPRECIATION.
*Thank them for sharing their thoughts with you.*

NANCY COBB AND CONNIE GRIGSBY
ADAPTED FROM "IS THERE A MOOSE IN YOUR MARRIAGE?"

# HOW TO TALK SO PEOPLE WILL LISTEN

BE CLEAR.
*Be specific and direct about*
*what you want to communicate.*

BE CONCISE.
*If you take too long to get to your point,*
*you will lose the other person's attention.*

BE CONSIDERATE.
*Treat your listener with courtesy and respect.*

BE CONSISTENT.
*Make sure your nonverbal message*
*is consistent with your verbal message.*
*Also, make sure your lifestyle*
*is consistent with what you say.*

BE COMFORTABLE.
*If you are nervous or uptight,*
*you will make others feel the same way.*

BE CREDIBLE.
*Make sure your facts are correct,*
*and be careful about exaggeration.*

DR. STEVE STEPHENS
PSYCHOLOGIST AND SEMINAR SPEAKER

# A PERSONAL MISSION STATEMENT...

...represents the deepest and best within you. It comes out of a solid connection with your inner life.

...is the fulfillment of your own unique gifts. It's the expression of your unique capacity to contribute.

...is transcendent. It's based on principles of contribution and purpose higher than self.

...addresses and integrates...fundamental human needs and capacities. It includes fulfillment in physical, social, mental, and spiritual dimensions.

...is based on principles that produce quality-of-life results. Both the end and the means are based on true principles.

...deals with both vision-based and principle-based values. It's not enough to have values without vision; you want to be good, but you also want to be good for something.

...deals with all the significant roles in your life. It represents a lifetime balance of persona, family, work, community—whatever roles you feel are yours to fill.

...is written to inspire you, not to impress anyone else. It communicates to you and inspires you on the most essential level.

HYRUM W. SMITH
CONDENSED FROM "WHAT MATTERS MOST: THE POWER OF LIVING YOUR VALUES"

# PEOPLE WHO HAVE IT TOGETHER HAVE...

- **Self-Awareness.**
  These people know who they are. They know their abilities and strengths, what they are capable of doing, and how to accomplish it.

- **Confidence.**
  They lack fear.

- **Self-Worth.**
  This is most often evidenced by their focus, not on themselves but on those they serve and work with.

- **A Sense of Urgency.**
  This means a "divine impatience" about everything they do.

- **A Strong Sense of Personal Mission.**
  There is a vision of what needs to be done and a passion and focus about doing it.

- **Awareness and Respect for Their Own Uniqueness.**
  They don't compare themselves to others or worry about what they're not. Their focus is on what they are.

- **A Consistency to Their Lives.**
  They are not tossed to and fro with every new idea or opportunity or change of events.

- **A Sense of Calmness and Serenity.**
  They are often people who can keep their heads when all about them are losing theirs.

HYRUM W. SMITH
CONDENSED FROM "WHAT MATTERS MOST: THE POWER OF LIVING YOUR VALUES"

# GREAT WAYS TO HELP OTHERS REACH THEIR GOALS

APPLAUD THE TINIEST OF SUCCESSES.

SHARE YOUR OWN EXPERIENCES.

TALK OFTEN ABOUT THEIR GOALS.

SUPPORT THEM DURING DIFFICULT TIMES.

SEND LETTERS AND NOTES OF ENCOURAGEMENT.

BUY LITTLE GIFTS AS REWARDS.

KEEP TRACK OF THEIR RECORD.

CYNDI HAYNES
FROM "THE BOOK OF CHANGE"

# HOW TO KEEP YOUR RESOLUTIONS

1. *Write them down.*
2. *Count the cost.*
3. *Make them meaningful.*
4. *Give them priority.*
5. *Be specific and practical.*
6. *Ask someone to keep you accountable.*
7. *Seek help if you struggle.*
8. *Break them into steps.*
9. *Reward yourself for each successful step.*
10. *Keep your eyes on the goal.*
11. *Do all you can to make them fun.*
12. *Pray.*

JOHN VAN DIEST
ASSOCIATE PUBLISHER

# THE TOP 10 MISTAKES LEADERS MAKE

1. **The Top-Down Attitude**
   The top-down attitude comes naturally to most people. It is based on the military model of barking orders to those beneath you. But effective leaders seek good ideas from all levels, thus empowering those below them.

2. **Putting Paperwork Before Peoplework**
   The greater the leadership role, the more important peoplework is. Only through association is there transformation.

3. **The Absence of Affirmation**
   Everyone thrives on affirmation and praise. We wildly underestimate the power of the tiniest personal touch of kindness. Learn to read the varying levels of affirmation your people need.

4. **No Room for Mavericks**
   Mavericks can save us from the slide toward institutionalism. They bring us the future! Learn to recognize truly useful mavericks.

5. **Dictatorship in Decision Making**
   Dictators deny the value of individuals. The major players in an organization are like its stockholders. They should have a say in its direction.

6. **Dirty Delegation**
   Overmanaging is one of the cardinal sins of poor leadership. Nothing frustrates those who work for you more than sloppy delegation with too many strings attached. Delegation should match each worker's follow-through ability.

7. **Communication Chaos**
   The bigger the group, the more attention that must be given to communication. Communication must be the passionate obsession of effective leadership.

8. **Missing the Clues of Corporate Culture**
   Every system has a set of values and beliefs. If we don't understand this culture, we create conflict, dissonance, and frustration.

9. **Success with Successors**
   Pride tightens the grip on leadership; humility relaxes and lets go. Letting go of leadership is like sending your children away to college: It hurts, but it has to be done. Mentoring is a non-negotiable function of successful leadership.

10. **Failure to Focus on the Future**
    The future is rushing at us at breakneck speed. A leader's concentration must not be on the past or on the present, but on the future. Vision is an effective leader's chief preoccupation.

HANS FINZEL
CONDENSED FROM "THE TOP TEN MISTAKES LEADERS MAKE"

# WHAT A LEADER DOES

1. Provides direction
2. Provides vision
3. Provides a character role model
4. Puts more value on people than on programs or ideas
5. Takes responsibility
6. Researches a situation before jumping to conclusions
7. Pushes others to exceed even beyond the abilities of the leader
8. Places an attitude of dignity and worth upon each individual
9. Affirms the positive in others
10. Motivates through…

*continuous training*
*encouragement and empowerment*
*allowing ownership*
*providing incentives and rewards*
*self-sacrifice*
*providing a leadership example*

JULIE BAKER
FROM "TIME OUT FOR WOMEN" MAGAZINE

# AM I TEACHABLE?

1. I am willing to listen more than talk.
2. I admit when I am mistaken.
3. I observe before acting on a situation.
4. I am able to agree to disagree.
5. I desire information more than answers.
6. I enjoy asking questions.
7. I am open to suggestions and new ideas.
8. I feel comfortable asking for advice or directions.
9. I am a patient and willing "student."
10. I enjoy reading for information that is practical and applicable.
11. I seek out new perspectives on the questions of life.
12. I can appreciate criticism without being deeply wounded.

MARTY WILLIAMS
PASTOR OF FAMILY MINISTRIES

# THOSE WHO ATTAIN THEIR GOALS ARE...

- PERSEVERING
- SPIRITUAL
- BOLD
- DETERMINED
- IMAGINATIVE
- DAUNTLESS
- PLUCKY
- CREATIVE
- SELF-RELIANT
- COURAGEOUS
- UNWAVERING
- UNCOMPROMISING
- CONFIDENT
- BRAVE

CYNDI HAYNES
FROM "THE BOOK OF CHANGE"

# PUT SPACE IN YOUR SCHEDULE

1. STOP.

   Take a little time every day to think—not just about what you're doing but also why you're doing it.

2. PREPARE.

   Prepare for the wrecks of life. Even when things go wrong, planning ahead can help us pick up the pieces and keep moving forward.

3. ADJUST YOUR ATTITUDE.

   Focus on the good in a situation.

4. CONCENTRATE.

   You must discern what your gifts are and what they are not. Say yes to the best, and don't rise up to everything others want you to do.

5. ENERGIZE.

   Engage in energy-renewing activities. The difference between space and stress is the difference between your limit and your load. If your load and limit are the same, you need to work on the limit, because sometimes you can't do much about the load.

CHARLES LOWERY
FROM "HOMELIFE" MAGAZINE

# CONQUER YOUR MOUNTAIN OF CLUTTER

BUILD WHITE SPACE INTO YOUR CALENDAR.

Don't schedule tasks to consume every working and waking moment. Plan for about 80-percent capacity. That means for a forty-hour workweek, schedule about thirty hours of work and know that another ten hours of "stuff" will appear unexpectedly.

BE WARY OF HIGH-TECH TIMESAVING DEVICES.

High-tech may mean high-time. Before buying any "timesaving" gadget, consider the hidden investment of time in its use: time to select and purchase it, time to learn how to operate it, time to set up and secure it, time to refurbish or repair it, and time to replace it.

CLUTTER YOUR TO-DO LIST, NOT YOUR MIND.

Your mind can hold only about seven chunks of information at once, so why push your luck? If you have flashes of brilliance when you're in the shower, out for a walk, or driving on the freeway, write them down immediately rather than trying to juggle them in your mind.

WORK IN MARATHONS.

Marathons serve two purposes: to catch up or to get ahead. When you feel as if you're slipping farther and farther behind, do a work marathon to catch up. Arrive early. Work late. Don't allow interruptions, and don't repeat anything. Work fast, and don't look up between tasks. Put in three or four days like that, and you'll feel caught up enough to face the world again.

COMPLETE THINGS.

Bonuses come upon the completion of projects. Signed contracts come at the end of negotiations. Points go on the scoreboard only when the runner crosses the goal line. One thing completed is worth ten things on hold. Incomplete tasks can make you feel depressed and wasted; you will feel energized after completing them.

DIANNA BOOHER
FROM "GET A LIFE WITHOUT SACRIFICING YOUR CAREER"

# GOLDEN THREADS OF A SUCCESSFUL LIFE

- People who know the most know that they know so little, while people who know nothing want to take all day to tell you about it.

- Self-improvement can be harmful if you are doing it to look better. If you live your life helping others look better, you'll become better without trying.

- If you give in order to get something, you're not really giving—you're trading.

- Big people are always giving someone credit and taking blame; little people are always seeking credit and giving blame.

- Don't worry about having to make a right decision. Make it and then work to make it right.

- An attitude of gratitude should flavor everything you do. Learning to be thankful is the golden thread woven through every truly successful life.

CHARLIE "TREMENDOUS" JONES
PRESIDENT, LIFE MANAGEMENT SERVICES, INC.
CONDENSED FROM "LIFE IS TREMENDOUS"

# SUCCESS PRINCIPLES
## (COLLECTED FROM IMPRESSIVE ENTREPRENEURS)

1. Earn trust by giving it. 2. Take responsibility for your actions. 3. Get the facts before making decisions. 4. Go the extra mile. 5. Put first things first and last things not at all. 6. Accentuate the positive. 7. Center your life around specific goals. 8. Devote yourself to lifelong learning. 9. Discover and follow your calling. 10. Concentrate on what you do well. 11. Pour a solid foundation of hard work. 12. Find your weaknesses and fix them. 13. Cultivate new shoots from old roots. 14. Live with passion! 15. Speak the truth in love. 16. Honor those in authority. 17. Start over if necessary. 18. Face life with boldness and courage. 19. Block out the unnecessary. 20. Conquer your personal demons. 21. Seek divine guidance. 22. Excel at helping others excel. 23. Care deeply about people. 24. Take risks with people. 25. Lighten up—you'll live longer. 26. Stay open to timely opportunities. 27. Surround yourself with experience. 28. Focus on what really matters in life. 29. Help others with what you've learned. 30. Escape the complacency that can come with success. 31. Follow your sense of calling, even to unexpected places. 32. Give your time and talents to causes you believe in. 33. Live for something bigger than you. 34. Open the door when opportunity knocks. 35. Envision the future you want to create. 36. Make positive values a forethought, not an afterthought. 37. Have a realistic time frame for your dreams. 38. Use your head to follow your heart. 39. Find a way around roadblocks. 40. Leave an indelible impact on those you serve. 41. Commit to a concept with a future. 42. Practice forgiveness as a way of life. 43. Turn disappointments into discoveries. 44. Lead from your values. 45. Maintain the tension between control and growth.

MERRILL OSTER AND MIKE HAMEL
CONDENSED FROM "THE ENTREPRENEUR'S CREED"

# NINE COMMUNICATION SKILLS

1. EYE COMMUNICATION:
the ability to make and maintain eye contact in a meaningful way.

2. GESTURE AND FACIAL EXPRESSION:
animation communicated through your face and body that corresponds with your message and conveys energy.

3. POSTURE AND MOVEMENT:
reflecting confidence and energy in your body position and movement.

4. DRESS AND APPEARANCE:
presenting yourself in a way that does not detract from the message you want your hearer to grasp.

5. VOICE AND VOCAL VARIETY:
employing pitch, volume, and vocal energy that will keep your listener engaged in the content of what you are saying.

6. WORDS AND FILLERS:

using language that is replete with meaning and effective pauses and devoid of "fillers"—those annoying "ums," "ahs," and meaningless phrases such as "whatever," "you know," "like," and "I mean."

7. HUMOR:

a healthy sense of humor about yourself and life in general that makes you approachable and likable.

8. LISTENER INVOLVEMENT:

simple ways to involve yourself with other listeners—whether one or one thousand—in order to help them listen.

9. THE "NATURAL SELF":

letting the real you come through without seeming stiff or phony.

BERT DECKER AND HERSHAEL W. YORK
FROM "SPEAKING WITH BOLD ASSURANCE: HOW TO BECOME A PERSUASIVE COMMUNICATOR"

# THE WAY TO SUCCESS

- *Think rightly.*
- *Feel deeply.*
- *Choose wisely.*
- *Act accordingly.*
- *Live intentionally.*

LOREN FISCHER
PROFESSOR AND PASTOR

# THE CREDIT BELONGS TO THE MAN WHO...

*strives valiantly.*

*knows great enthusiasms and great devotions.*

*spends himself in a worthy cause.*

*at the best knows the triumph of high achievement.*

*at the worst fails while daring greatly.*

THEODORE ROOSEVELT
THE TWENTY-SIXTH PRESIDENT OF THE UNITED STATES

# FRIENDSHIP

*Developing a heart for others*

2

# 10 THINGS FRIENDS COMMUNICATE

1. COMFORT: *easing grief or pain.*
2. ATTENTION: *being thoughtful.*
3. ACCEPTANCE: *receiving in spite of faults.*
4. APPRECIATION: *showing gratefulness and praise.*
5. SUPPORT: *helping to carry another's burden.*
6. ENCOURAGEMENT: *urging or inspiring toward a goal.*
7. AFFECTION: *demonstrating care through touch or words.*
8. RESPECT: *valuing and esteeming.*
9. SECURITY: *protecting one from harm, fear, or loss.*
10. APPROVAL: *affirming your friend.*

DAVID AND TERESA FERGUSON
ADAPTED FROM "NEVER ALONE"

# FIVE GREAT WAYS TO FIND A FRIEND

1. **Find a cause.**

   Get involved in a worthwhile project that tugs at your heart. You'll find people there with a similar heart. And you'll accomplish something meaningful in the midst of your friendship hunt.

2. **Find a church.**

   Get plugged into a church that believes as you do. Be sure you make it to the small groups and the extra activities offered for your age group—even if you're shy.

3. **Find a class.**

   Aerobics, crafts, and college-credit courses all offer a place to meet people with common interests, which makes it easier to strike up conversation and build a friendship.

4. **Find a club.**

   Play groups and other organized functions for children can help you find friends while your kids do, too.

5. **Find a committee.**

   If you have good leadership skills, jumping into a job in a church or civic organization is a wonderful way to connect. Working side by side with people can forge close friendships while accomplishing a worthy objective.

RHONDA RHEA
CONDENSED FROM "TODAY'S CHRISTIAN WOMAN" MAGAZINE

# ARE YOU TOO SENSITIVE?

- Do your feelings get hurt more than once a day?
- Do you want to "get even" with people who hurt your feelings?
- Do you hold onto grudges longer than a day?
- Do you readily accept the apologies of those who offend you?
- Do you pout?
- Do you withdraw from your "offender"?
- Do you give your offender the silent treatment?
- Do you sometimes forget why you got mad in the first place?
- Do you let others' treatment of you affect the way you treat them?
- Do you withhold forgiveness until the one who hurt you apologizes?
- Do little hurts bother you?
- Do you become defensive regarding constructive criticism?
- Do people have to tread lightly around you?
- Do you prefer to think of yourself as a sensitive person?

NANCY COBB AND CONNIE GRIGSBY
FROM "HOW TO GET YOUR HUSBAND TO TALK TO YOU"

# THE ABC'S OF FRIENDSHIP

*A Friend…*

**A**ccepts you as you are.

**B**elieves in you.

**C**alls you just to say "hi."

**D**oesn't give up on you.

**E**nvisions the whole of you, even the unfinished parts.

**F**orgives your mistakes.

**G**ives unconditionally.

**H**elps you.

**I**nvites you over to…

**J**ust "be" with you.

**K**eeps you close at heart.

**L**oves you for who you are.

**M**akes a difference in your life.

Never judges.

Offers support.

Picks you up.

Quiets your fears.

Raises your spirits.

Says nice things about you.

Tells you the truth when you need to hear it.

Understands you.

Values you.

Walks beside you.

X-plains when you won't listen.

Zaps you back to reality!

AUTHOR UNKNOWN

# HOW TO BE FRIENDLY TO YOUR NEIGHBORS

1. **Introduce yourself.**
   Greeting your neighbors (and their children) by name is the first step in building community.

2. **Don't give your neighbors a reason to grumble.**
   Keep your lawn neat and litter free. If you have pets, clean up after them. If you have children, make sure they don't invade your neighbors' space.

3. **When possible, practice tolerance.**
   Is it really that big a deal if your neighbor's dog chases a squirrel into your yard? Resist the temptation to let things come before people.

4. **Share the bounty.**
   If you're making meals for the week or doing some baking, make a little extra for a busy mother or single person.

5. **Notice things.**
   Admire the new geraniums in their yard, or the A on little Jimmy's school paper.

6. **Celebrate occasions big and small.**
   Leave a small flowering plant on the doorstep on the first day of spring, a balloon (perhaps with a string tied around a candy bar) for a child's birthday.

KIM BOYCE AND HEIDI HESS SAXTON
FROM "TOUCHED BY KINDNESS"

# WHEN IN CRISIS, FIND GOOD FRIENDS WHO...

- Don't shock easily, but accept your human feelings. Are not embarrassed by your tears.
- Do not give unwanted advice.
- Are warm and affectionate with you according to your needs.
- Help you recall your strengths when you have forgotten that you have strengths.
- Trust you to be able to come through this difficult time.
- Treat you like an adult who can make your own decisions.
- May become angry with you but do not attack your character.
- Respect your courage and sense of determination.
- Understand that grief is normal and understand the stages of grief.
- Have been through times of difficulty and can share those times with you.
- Try to understand what your feelings mean to you.
- Are faithful to commitments and promises.
- Pray with you and for you.

ANN KAISER STEARNS
REPRINTED FROM "LIVING THROUGH PERSONAL CRISIS"

# FIVE PRINCIPLES FOR AUTHENTIC COMMUNICATION

1.
Communication problems are usually heart problems.

2.
Your ears are your most important communication tools.

3.
Good communication doesn't happen by accident.

4.
The absence of conflict doesn't equal good communication.

5.
Motive is more important than technique.

JOSHUA HARRIS
CONDENSED FROM "BOY MEETS GIRL"

# MUTUAL EXCHANGE

Friendship involves the mutual exchange of...

- *knowledge*
- *kindness*
- *service*
- *celebration*

JOHN ORTBERG, JUDSON POLING, AND LAURIE PEDERSON
FROM "GROUPS: THE LIFE-GIVING POWER OF COMMUNITY"

# LOVING IDEAS

- Don't underestimate the simple act of smiling.

- Be friendly, polite, and liberal with *please, thank you,* and sincere words of affirmation.

- Really listen. Look people in the eye, and give them your full attention.

- Refrain from judging. Give others the benefit of the doubt. Help others live up to your good expectations of them.

- Learn to say "I'm sorry" with sincerity and humility.

- Treat every call as if it is the most important one of the day. Let both your tone and your words say "Welcome," not "Keep out."

- When someone expresses a need, do something about it.

- Be prompt with get-well cards and expressions of sympathy.
- Share what you already have: home-baked bread, garden produce, outgrown clothing and toys, extra furniture.
- Teach a skill to a younger person.
- Remember birthdays and anniversaries with a card.
- If you have the time and the stamina, offer to baby-sit occasionally for single moms or just plain hassled and harried moms.
- Send thank-you notes promptly after receiving a gift or special help.
- Love generously.

LINDA RILEY
CONDENSED FROM "THE CALL TO LOVE"

# UNDERSTANDING FRIENDSHIP

*Friendship is a sheltering tree.*
SAMUEL TAYLOR COLERIDGE

*A friend is someone who understands your past,*
*believes in your future,*
*and accepts you just the way you are.*
AUTHOR UNKNOWN

*A true friend is a forever friend.*
GEORGE MACDONALD

*Treasures are not friends, but a friend is a treasure.*
FRENCH SAYING

*Friendship is one of the sweetest joys of life.*
*Many might have fallen beneath the bitterness of*
*their trial had they not found a friend.*
CHARLES SPURGEON

*My best friend is the one who brings out the best in me.*

HENRY FORD

*Two are better than one,*
*because they have a good return for their work:*
*If one falls down, his friend can help him up.*
*But pity the man who falls and has no one to help him up!*

ECCLESIASTES 4:9–10
FROM "THE HOLY BIBLE"

*A friend is someone who sees through you and still enjoys the view.*

WILMA ASKINAS

*A friend will strengthen you with her prayers,*
*bless you with her love, and encourage you with her heart.*

AUTHOR UNKNOWN

# SINCERE FRIENDS...

*Know my feelings.*

*Reveal to me how they feel.*

*Teach me about myself.*

*Are comfortable with silence.*

*Feel free to tell me the truth.*

*Give me freedom to fail.*

*Love me for who I am.*

SHERI ROSE SHEPHERD
FROM "FIT FOR EXCELLENCE"

# SUPERFICIAL FRIENDS...

*Know only the facts about me.*

*Tell me what they've done.*

*Tell me about others.*

*Feel awkward with silence.*

*Would leave me if I let them down.*

*Love me for what I can do.*

SHERI ROSE SHEPHERD
FROM "FIT FOR EXCELLENCE"

# THE NATURE OF FRIENDSHIP

***Friends can say almost anything.***

Friends feel safe with friends. You know you can be yourself.

***Friends keep confidences.***

I keep yours; you keep mine. There's never the fear that something will be used against us.

***Friends counsel.***

When the rest of the world doesn't care that we're about to die inside, a friend does: "I love you and I'm with you"; "You need to stop drinking"; "You really need to watch spending too much time with that person."

***Friends listen.***

The flip side of that last coin is that we know that our friends have our best interests at heart when they counsel us, and we listen.

*Friends sacrifice.*

Just as a friend is willing to take risks on our behalf, a friend often makes sacrifices for a friend.

***Friends have no hidden agendas.***

Friends work to have no hidden jealousies, desires, angers, or barriers of any kind that come between them and their friend. Friendship is built on honesty.

*Friends are always there.*

If your friend needs to talk, no matter what hour of the day or night, you're there to talk.

*Friends have fun together.*

They kid around, joke, play, have a host of inside jokes and use them frequently, and generally enjoy just being with one another—no matter what they're doing.

TIM AND JULIE CLINTON
CONDENSED FROM "THE MARRIAGE YOU'VE ALWAYS WANTED"

# HOW TO HELP A FRIEND WHO IS DEPRESSED

## BE THERE

You don't have to say a lot. In fact, people who are depressed are not good conversationalists. Don't ask a lot of questions. Depressed folks have enough questions without trying to answer yours, too. You are there to listen, to help your friend vent his or her frustrations and doubts, and to provide a spirit of encouragement.

## DON'T PREACH

The last thing a depressed person needs is a sermon. However, sharing an uplifting Scripture may be appropriate.

## LOVE UNCONDITIONALLY

Depressed people are often incapable of loving themselves. Expressions of love and affection, either verbal or written, are important to those who are recovering from depression. They need to know they will not be abandoned regardless of their emotional condition.

## ENCOURAGE

Let your depressed friend know how much you believe in him or her. Reinforce his or her good qualities. Remind the person of his or her strengths.

## TRY TO ENGAGE IN ACTIVITY

Don't give him or her a choice. Call on the spur of the moment and say, "We're going fishing—I'll meet you." Or, "Let's have lunch—I'll pick you up in thirty minutes." Don't give the depressed person time to think about whether or not he or she can participate in an activity. If you give him or her a choice, it'll be "No!" every time.

## PRAY

Pray with and/or for the depressed person. It can make a huge difference.

STAN TOLER AND DEBRA WHITE SMITH
CONDENSED FROM "THE HARDER I LAUGH, THE DEEPER I HURT"

# YOUR BEST FRIEND

A FRIEND sees the best in you, even when you're not showing it.

A FRIEND knows when you need someone to talk to, when you need to be alone, and, most important, the difference between the two.

A FRIEND can tell when you need a hug and doesn't hesitate to offer one.

A FRIEND makes you laugh when you see little to laugh about.

A FRIEND will always come to your defense, no matter how often called upon to do it or how unpopular it makes her or him.

A FRIEND believes you first and rumors second.

A FRIEND never passes up the chance to encourage you.

A FRIEND shares with you, even chocolate.

A FRIEND tells you when you're about to make a mistake.

A FRIEND is someone you can always depend on, even when you don't deserve it.

A FRIEND brings out the best in you, but doesn't insist on the credit.

A FRIEND understands you, even when you don't.

MARTHA BOLTON
FROM "I LOVE YOU...STILL"

# VIRTUE

3

*Honing a character of goodness*

# RIPPLES OF LOVE

Love is always building up.

It puts some line of beauty on everything it touches.

It gives new hope to discouraged ones,
new strength to those who are weak.

It helps the despairing to rise and start again.

It makes life seem more worthwhile to everyone
into whose eyes it looks.

Its words are benedictions.

Its every breath is full of inspiration.

AUTHOR UNKNOWN

# DO LESS

- DO LESS THINKING,
  *and pay more attention to your heart.*

- DO LESS ACQUIRING,
  *and pay more attention to what you already have.*

- DO LESS COMPLAINING,
  *and pay more attention to giving.*

- DO LESS CONTROLLING,
  *and pay more attention to letting go.*

- DO LESS CRITICIZING,
  *and pay more attention to complimenting.*

- DO LESS ARGUING,
  *and pay more attention to forgiveness.*

- DO LESS RUNNING AROUND,
  *and pay more attention to stillness.*

- DO LESS TALKING,
  *and pay more attention to silence.*

LEE L. JAMPOLSKY
REPRINTED FROM "SMILE FOR NO GOOD REASON"

# SOLITUDE IS A PLACE WHERE...

*Meaning is found.*

*Truth is pondered.*

*Convictions are solidified.*

*Inspiration is born.*

*Visions are cast.*

*Character is developed.*

*Humility is learned.*

*Wrongs are forgiven.*

*Virtues are sought.*

*Demons are conquered.*

*Peace is embraced.*

*Love is nurtured.*

*Faith is enlarged.*

*Healing is discovered.*

*Joy is planted.*

DR. STEVE STEPHENS
PSYCHOLOGIST AND SEMINAR SPEAKER

# BETTER YOUR LIFE

1.
Avoid gossip.

2.
Release bitterness.

3.
Take risks.

4.
Trust.

5.
Don't live for "stuff."

6.
Master your appetites.

7.
Grow deep.

8.
Be generous.

9.
Think globally.

PAUL BORTHWICK
SENIOR CONSULTANT, DEVELOPMENT ASSOCIATES INTERNATIONAL
FROM "DISCIPLESHIP JOURNAL"

# EVERY NIGHT WE SHOULD ASK OURSELVES...

*What infirmity have I mastered today?*

*What passions have I opposed?*

*What temptation have I resisted?*

*What virtue have I acquired?*

SENECA
PHILOSOPHER AND PLAYWRIGHT

# A MATURITY TEST

1. Do you tend to blame other people when things go wrong?
2. Do you make excuses for your failures?
3. Do you prefer to ignore difficulties and hope they'll go away on their own?
4. Do you sometimes blame your poor background for why you've never fulfilled your potential?
5. Do you tell a little white lie if it will get you off the hook?
6. Do people sometimes say, "When are you ever going to grow up?"
7. Do you avoid responsibility if possible?

8. Do you find it difficult to adjust to new situations?

9. Do you wonder if you'll ever get all of your life together?

10. Do you often think—or tell others—that next year will be different, better, a success?

11. Are you usually able to talk your way out of most anything?

12. Do you feel that you never get the breaks you deserve?

13. When you're caught at something you shouldn't be doing, is your first thought to lie or make excuses?

14. Do you feel that if you had a bigger or better house you'd be happy?

FLORENCE AND FRED LITTAUER
FROM "AFTER EVERY WEDDING COMES A MARRIAGE"

# BLESSED ARE THOSE WHO...

- Do what is right.
- Speak the truth with compassion.
- Treat their neighbors with love and respect.
- Avoid those who do wrong and cling to those who do right.
- Keep their commitments even when it hurts.
- Conduct every transaction with fairness and honor.

KING DAVID
PARAPHRASED FROM PSALM 15

# THE FACES OF LOVE

JOY *is love exalted.*

PEACE *is love in repose.*

LONG-SUFFERING *is love enduring.*

GENTLENESS *is love in society.*

GOODNESS *is love in action.*

FAITH *is love on the battlefield.*

MEEKNESS *is love in school.*

TEMPERANCE *is love in training.*

DWIGHT L. MOODY
PASTOR AND EVANGELIST

# GREED AND GENEROSITY

| | |
|---|---|
| GREED *is self-centered.* | GENEROSITY *is other-focused.* |
| GREED *hoards.* | GENEROSITY *helps.* |
| GREED *holds a tight grip.* | GENEROSITY *shares freely.* |
| GREED *is closefisted.* | GENEROSITY *is openhanded.* |
| GREED *keeps mental lists of wants.* | GENEROSITY *keeps mental lists of people and projects that need assistance.* |

ED YOUNG
REPRINTED FROM "FATAL DISTRACTIONS"

# THE VIRTUE OF DISCIPLINE

1.
DISCIPLINES OF LIFESTYLE
*Establish a life of simplicity.*
*Do what you can to reduce meaningless activity.*

2.
DISCIPLINES OF THE WHOLE PERSON
*Once steps toward a simpler life are taken,*
*we can live a life of joy when focusing on what*
*we feed our mind; how we exercise;*
*and how we rest our mind, body, and spirit.*

3.
DISCIPLINES OF LABOR
*People who greatly enjoy life tend to be those*
*who are involved in the disciplines of service*
*and meaningful work balanced with fun.*

LINDSEY O'CONNOR
FROM "IF MAMA AIN'T HAPPY, AIN'T NOBODY HAPPY"

*Deep optimism is aware of problems,*
*but recognizes the solutions;*
*knows about difficulties,*
*but believes they can be overcome;*
*sees the negative,*
*but accentuates the positive;*
*is exposed to the worst,*
*but expects the best;*
*has reason to complain,*
*but prefers to smile.*
WILLIAM ARTHUR WARD

*One man with courage is a majority.*
ANDREW JACKSON

*Faith sees the invisible,*
*believes the unbelievable,*
*and receives the impossible.*
CORRIE TEN BOOM

*Nothing in the world can take the place of persistence.*
CALVIN COOLIDGE

*May God grant us the wisdom*
*to discover the right,*
*the will to choose it,*
*and the strength*
*to make it endure.*
KING ARTHUR
FROM THE MOVIE "FIRST KNIGHT"

*Of two evils, choose neither.*
CHARLES SPURGEON

# A QUESTION OF CHARACTER

- Character is a CHOICE.
- Character means COMMITMENT.
- Character always CATCHES UP.
- Character creates PASSION.

THAD A. GAEBELEIN AND RON P. SIMMONS
CONDENSED FROM "A QUESTION OF CHARACTER"

# LIVING TO THE FULLEST

If you want to go far in life, be...

- *tender with the young,*
- *compassionate with the aged,*
- *sympathetic with the striving,*
- *tolerant of the weak and the strong.*

Because someday you will have been all of these.

GEORGE WASHINGTON CARVER
EDUCATOR AND SCIENTIST

# CODE OF CHARACTER

LOYALTY

DUTY

RESPECT

SELFLESS SERVICE

HONOR

INTEGRITY

PERSONAL COURAGE

MAJOR SCOTT BUCHMANN
PROFESSOR OF MILITARY SCIENCE OF THE U.S. ARMY

# THREE LEVELS OF KINDNESS

KINDNESS IN WORDS...
*creates confidence.*

KINDNESS IN THINKING...
*creates profoundness.*

KINDNESS IN GIVING...
*creates love.*

CHINESE PROVERB

# PEACEABLE LIVING

**Be True to Self:**

- Keep a clear conscience.
- Recognize weaknesses.
- Know strengths.
- Don't compare your weaknesses to others strengths.

**Attempt to Resolve Conflicts:**

- Be quick to go to the offended person.
- Communicate clearly, giving facts, feelings, and intuitions.
- Make no assumptions that the other person had additional information.
- Look for strengths in others instead of focusing on their weaknesses.

**Forgive:**

- Gain the freedom to learn, grow, and mature.
- Acknowledge that there is room for growth.
- Rid yourself of guilt, anger, and bitterness.
- Allow yourself the freedom to care deeply, to have compassion, and to love.

GLENDA HOTTON, MA
COUNSELOR

# HEALTH

*Nurturing a long and satisfying life*

4

SEVEN STEPS TO GREATER HEALTH

10 COMMANDMENTS OF GREAT NUTRITION

SAFETY TIPS FROM YOUR PHARMACIST

14 WAYS TO GET UP ON THE RIGHT SIDE OF THE BED

GETTING BETTER SLEEP

FIVE WAYS TO REDUCE STRESS

EIGHT STEPS FOR HEALTHFUL WALKING

WORKOUT REWARDS

ANGER-MANAGEMENT SKILLS

HEALTHY ANGER

HELP FOR HEADACHES

THE SYMPTOMS OF MENOPAUSE

TIPS FOR DEALING WITH HOT FLASHES

EATING RIGHT

SEVEN WAYS TO TAKE A DAILY MINIVACATION

HAVING A HEALTHY RETIREMENT

10 COMMANDMENTS FOR FITNESS

12 SYMPTOMS YOU SHOULD NEVER IGNORE

# SEVEN STEPS TO GREATER HEALTH

1.
Peaceful living

2.
Pure food

3.
Proper exercise

4.
Plenty of water

5.
Prayer and fasting

6.
Periods of fresh air and sunshine

7.
Perfect rest

STORMIE O'MARTIAN
FROM "GREATER HEALTH GOD'S WAY"

# 10 COMMANDMENTS OF GREAT NUTRITION

I. Thou shalt never skip breakfast.

II. Thou shalt eat every three to four hours.

III. Thou shalt always eat a carbohydrate with a protein.

IV. Thou shalt double your fiber.

V. Thou shalt trim the fat from your diet.

VI. Thou shalt believe your mother was right:
Eat your fruits and vegetables.

VII. Thou shalt get your vitamins from food, not pills.

VIII. Thou shalt drink at least eight glasses of water a day.

IX. Thou shalt consume a minimum of sugar, salt, caffeine, and alcohol.

X. Thou shalt never, never go on a fad diet!

WALTER BORTZ II, MD
FROM "WE LIVE TOO SHORT AND DIE TOO LONG"

# SAFETY TIPS FROM YOUR PHARMACIST

- Use child-resistant caps, and do not leave medicine uncapped.
- Store medicine as directed and in a safe place out of children's reach.
- Don't give medicine to children unless it is recommended for them on the label or by a doctor.
- Don't take medicine prescribed for anyone else or give your medication to others.
- Don't use medicine for purposes not mentioned on the container or in package directions, unless instructed by a doctor.
- Don't try to remember the dose used during previous illnesses; read the label each time.
- Keep liquid medicines in the original bottles; don't transfer to other containers.
- Used prescribed medicine for as long as the doctor recommends to ensure complete recovery.
- Check with your doctor or pharmacist if you have any problems with or questions about your medicine.

FOOD AND DRUG ADMINISTRATION

# 14 WAYS TO GET UP ON THE RIGHT SIDE OF THE BED

1.
Stretch your arms and legs.

2.
Take four big healthy yawns.

3.
Say a prayer.

4.
Push back the sheets and jump out of bed.

5.
Take a shower.

6.
Look forward to something.

7.
Exercise for at least five minutes.

8.
Brush your teeth.

9.
Think positively.

10.
Take a walk.

11.
Breathe deeply.

12.
Enjoy a hot cup of coffee, tea, or hot chocolate.

13.
Consider who you can encourage today.

14.
Thank God for the sunshine and the rain and that you have the strength to appreciate whatever the day will bring.

BECKY STEPHENS
REGISTERED NURSE

# GETTING BETTER SLEEP

1\.

AVOID THE TEMPTATION TO SLEEP IN ON THE WEEKENDS.

Going to bed at the same time every evening and waking up at the same time every morning will help establish good sleeping habits.

2\.

TURN THAT TELEVISION OFF!

A noisy room usually leads to less restful sleep. Also, stimulating your brain just before bedtime makes it harder to leave behind the day and its tensions.

3\.

DON'T NAP TO MAKE UP FOR LOST SLEEP.

If you're napping to make up for last night's lack of sleep, you may be interfering with tonight's sleep. It's better to arrive at bedtime thoroughly tired.

4.

EXERCISE—BUT DON'T DO IT CLOSE TO BEDTIME.

When done regularly, exercise can improve your overall sleep. But if you exercise within two hours of bedtime, you'll likely be too keyed up to fall asleep.

5.

CAFFEINE IS A STIMULANT.

I've learned that I can't drink coffee after noon unless I want to be awake until the wee hours of the morning. Your body may respond differently. But if you're having trouble getting to sleep, try avoiding caffeine.

AMY GIVLER, MD
FROM "HOMELIFE" MAGAZINE

# FIVE WAYS TO REDUCE STRESS

1.

**ASSESS HOW STRESS IMPACTS YOUR LIFE.**

Identify the time of day during which you feel the most tension. Recognize how your body responds to stress. Does your neck get stiff? Does your stomach churn? Becoming aware of the ways in which stress affects you is the first step in dealing with its negative influences.

2.

**PRIORITIZE.**

What's really important? Do you want to simplify the daily schedule? Write down your ideas at the top of the calendar. This visual reminder will help you say no to activities and commitments that aren't important.

3.

**BE REALISTIC.**

Stress is part of everyone's life. Remembering that you aren't the only one who faces stress will help put issues into a broader perspective.

4.

**CELEBRATE WORKABLE COPING TECHNIQUES.**

Do you feel tension slip away during a daily walk? Do you relax over a cup of tea? Make a list of ways you effectively manage stress. Post the list on the refrigerator. Then, the next time you respond too sharply to someone or yell at the dog, glance at your list and say, "Maybe it's time for a cup of tea!"

5.

**BE KIND TO YOURSELF.**

Children aren't the only ones who benefit from a "time-out." Give yourself permission from time to time to take a bubble bath or read a good book.

MARY MANZ SIMON
CONDENSED FROM "THE YEAR-ROUND PARENT"

# EIGHT STEPS FOR HEALTHFUL WALKING

1. Check with your doctor before starting.
2. Wear shoes that are comfortable and specifically designed for walking.
3. Carry a MedicAlert card listing any specific health concerns, such as diabetes or heart problems.
4. Pace yourself as you begin a walking program.
5. Walk erect, with your head and neck as much in line with your spine as possible.
6. Walk slightly faster than normal in order to gradually raise your heart rate sensibly and without stress.
7. Watch for uneven sidewalks, curbs, and dips or breaks in sidewalks that could cause you to fall.
8. On extremely hot or rainy days, travel to a nearby mall for your walk.

GEORGE L. BAKER
CONDENSED FROM "LIFEWISE" MAGAZINE

# WORKOUT REWARDS

1.
INCREASED ENERGY
Exercise stretches the lungs, dilates blood vessels, and allows blood to flow more freely.

2.
CARDIOVASCULAR CONDITIONING
Exercise strengthens the heart.

3.
HIGHER METABOLISM
Exercise burns fat faster.

4.
INCREASED BRAIN FUNCTION
Exercise improves circulation to the brain.

5.
STRESS-BUSTER
Exercise is an effective stress-buster, reenergizing the body and acting as a safety valve for our roiling internal anxieties.

6.
FLUIDITY OF MOVEMENT
Exercise also alleviates stiffness and rigidity, which in turn cuts down on injury from moving or lifting.

SHIRLEY MITCHELL
CONDENSED FROM "FABULOUS AFTER 50"

# ANGER-MANAGEMENT SKILLS

1. *Remember that feeling angry isn't wrong.* Expressing that anger in unproductive and hurtful ways is!

2. *Learn to defuse your angry energy through relaxation.* Learn to relax by using deep-breathing techniques and by picturing pleasant thoughts.

3. *Work off the excess energy.* Strenuous activity or exercise is an excellent tool for ridding yourself of pent-up tension and energy that could be released as anger.

4. *Talk yourself through your anger.* Often it's the running dialogue that goes on in our heads that fuels the anger we feel. But you can turn the table by learning to "talk yourself through" your anger.

5. *"Use your words"—positively.* Learn to express your attitudes, expectations, desires, and even your angry feelings directly and verbally instead of blowing up in frustration or expecting others to read your mind.

6. *Learn to express your feelings without assigning blame.* This will not only make a difference in your own mind; it will help keep the situation from escalating.

7. *Go slow and soft.* When in a heated conversation, slow down your speaking (literally) and soften your voice. It's difficult to explode when you're speaking in soft, restrained tones.

8. *Lighten up and laugh!* Sometimes we'd rather roll over and die before admitting to the humor of a stressful situation.

9. *Back off on the sarcasm.* Don't forget that sarcastic and hurtful "humor" can be simply a passive-aggressive form of anger.

10. *Journal your emotions of anger.* Consider your journal a safe, no-holds-barred place to vent—as well as a place to brainstorm creative solutions to anger-producing circumstances.

11. *Think ahead about anger-producing situations.* Prepare yourself mentally for circumstances that tend to push your buttons—and plan some strategies for defusing these situations.

12. *In calm moments, focus on creative problem solving.* Strategize about ways you could rearrange your life to avoid circumstances that tick you off.

13. *Don't overlook the possible need for help with anger issues.* A counselor with expertise in anger management can help. So can enrolling in a seminar or workshop on assertiveness training.

14. *Don't forget to give yourself an occasional time-out!* Sometimes the best response to emotional situations is just to count to ten and wait things out.

JULIE ANN BARNHILL
CONDENSED FROM "SHE'S GONNA BLOW!"

# HEALTHY ANGER

*Healthy anger happens when it is expressed…*

- with the right PERSON
- to the right DEGREE
- at the right TIME
- for the right PURPOSE
- in the right WAY

ARISTOTLE
ADAPTED FROM "NICOMACHEAN ETHICS"

# HELP FOR HEADACHES

1.
Let your doctor know you have them.

2.
Make an appointment specifically about your headaches.
Headaches are a legitimate medical disorder.

3.
Bring a list of current medications.
Include all over-the-counter products
and any natural supplements.

4.
Prepare for a dialogue with your physician.
Be organized, specific, direct, and ready to talk "details."

5.
Be proactive. Ask questions.
Work with your doctor to choose
the treatment that's right for you.

AMY GIVLER, MD
CONDENSED FROM "HOMELIFE" MAGAZINE

# THE SYMPTOMS OF MENOPAUSE

Menstrual irregularity

Hot flashes and night sweats

Sleep disturbances

Fatigue

Emotional symptoms

Joint pain

Vaginal dryness

ROBERT WELLS, MD, AND MARY WELLS
CONDENSED FROM "MENOPAUSE AND MID-LIFE"

# TIPS FOR DEALING WITH HOT FLASHES

- Layer your clothing so that you can remove the outer layer when a hot flash occurs.
- Choose natural fabrics, such as cotton and wool, which help you stay cool.
- Place a cool cloth or ice pack on your face during a hot flash to counter the warmth.
- Sip ice water.
- Avoid caffeine and alcohol, which tend to raise your body temperature. Also avoid sugar.
- Stay away from such triggers as spicy foods, overheated rooms, hot beverages, and stress.

SELECTED FROM "ABOUT...MENOPAUSE," A LIFE ADVICE® PAMPHLET
PUBLISHED BY METLIFE'S CONSUMER EDUCATION CENTER

# EATING RIGHT

1.

**Aim for a healthful weight.**

*In addition to watching your weight,
keep your waist measurement below thirty-five inches (for women)
or forty inches (for men).*

2.

**Be physically active each day.**

*Our body functions best when it's used to moving.*

3.

**Let the food pyramid guide your choices.**

*An easy way to remember is that the bulk of your diet
should consist of grains, fruits, and vegetables.*

4.

**Choose a variety of grains daily, especially whole grains.**

*Eat breads and cereals made from whole grains.*

5.

**Choose a variety of fruits and vegetables daily.**

*Canned or frozen fruits or vegetables are great choices
if fresh produce isn't available.*

6.

**Keep food safe to eat.**

*Keep raw food separated from cooked food.*
*Be sure the refrigerator stays colder than forty degrees.*

7.

**Choose a diet low in saturated fat and cholesterol while moderate in total fat.**

*No more than 30 percent of your calories should come from fat, and only 10 percent should come from saturated fat.*

8.

**Choose beverages and foods to moderate your intake of sugars.**

*Soft drinks are the leading source of added sugar in the American diet.*

9.

**Choose and prepare foods with herbs, and use less salt.**

AMY GIVLER, MD
FROM "HOMELIFE" MAGAZINE

# SEVEN WAYS TO TAKE A DAILY MINIVACATION

1.
Smile.

2.
Relax in a rocking chair.

3.
Breathe deeply.

4.
Alternate activities.

5.
Take a long, hot bath.

6.
Snuggle in a bathrobe while reading a good book.

7.
Listen to your favorite classical music
while sipping a cup of coffee.

JANE JARRELL
CONDENSED FROM "MOM MATTERS"

# HAVING A HEALTHY RETIREMENT

- Eat a balanced diet, including five helpings of fruits and vegetables each day.
- Exercise regularly.
- Get regular health checkups.
- Don't smoke.
- Practice safety habits at home to prevent falls and fractures. Always wear a seat belt in the car.
- Stay in contact with family and friends. Stay active through work, play, and community.
- Avoid overexposure to sun and cold.
- If you drink, moderation is the key. When you drink, let someone else drive.
- Keep personal and financial records in order to simplify budgeting and investing. Plan long-term housing and financial needs.
- Keep a positive attitude toward life. Do things that make you happy.

NATIONAL INSTITUTE OF AGING
FROM "MAJOR SENIOR MALADIES TO HEALTHY LIVING"

# 10 COMMANDMENTS FOR FITNESS

I.

RECOGNIZE THE LIMITATIONS OF YOUR BODY

It isn't as young as it used to be.

II.

KNOW YOUR GOALS

Set reasonable, reachable goals for your exercise program.

III.

KNOW YOUR BODY IN DETAIL

Treat it well, with proper nutrition and exercise.

IV.

KNOW YOUR SPORT

Its requirements, risks, benefits, preparatory training,
and protective measures.

V.

PREPARE

Start easily and build into activity.
Warm up and cool down. Stretch out. Cross-train.

VI.

KNOW THE MOST COMMON INJURIES

And know the signs of overtraining.

## VII.
## KNOW THE CURE

Injuries should be treated early and aggressively
to prevent degenerative changes from occurring and
to ensure a speedy return to activity.

## VIII.
## DON'T IGNORE AN INJURY

And don't try to be your own doctor.
Remember that rehabilitation can prevent reinjury.

## IX.
## SEEK OUT EXPERT ADVICE

Consult your physician, a trainer, a sports-medicine practitioner, a professional in your sport, or an organization dedicated to your sport.

## X.
## HAVE FUN

Relax. Enjoy. That's what it's all about.

ANDREW SEDDON, MD
FROM "STAYING FIT AFTER FORTY"

# 12 SYMPTOMS YOU SHOULD NEVER IGNORE

1. Unplanned, continuing weight loss
2. Persistent and intense headaches
3. Chest pain
4. Abdominal pain
5. Easy bruising and bleeding
6. Breathing problems
7. Unexplained depression
8. Suicidal feelings
9. Bumps or lumps that you didn't used to have
10. Persistent numbness
11. High blood pressure
12. Loss of consciousness (for any reason)

KEVIN MCCURRY, MD
FAMILY PHYSICIAN

# MARRIAGE AND ROMANCE

5

*Enjoying the best*

# WHAT MARRIAGE ISN'T

- *Marriage isn't the History Channel.* Old battles don't need to be revisited on a regular basis.
- *Marriage isn't a theatrical performance.* Substance counts more than show.
- *Marriage isn't a political rally.* Don't make promises you can't keep.
- *Marriage isn't a computer.* There's no limit to the amount of good memories you can store.
- *Marriage isn't an automobile.* You don't trade in your old model for a new one every hundred thousand miles.
- *Marriage isn't a competition.* If your partner wins, you win. If your partner loses, you both lose.
- *Marriage isn't an amusement park.* You don't exit as soon as the fun comes to a stop. It's a relationship you believe in enough to stick around until the fun returns.

MARTHA BOLTON
CONDENSED FROM "STILL THE ONE"

# ARE YOU A GREAT MARRIAGE PARTNER?

1. Do you give your spouse a hug or kiss each morning?
2. Do you look for opportunities to express your love?
3. Do you surprise your spouse with compliments and gifts?
4. Do you let go of passing annoyances or differences that could turn into conflicts?
5. Do you periodically do it his or her way instead of your way?
6. Do you take the time to have heart-to-heart chats?
7. Do you truly listen to your spouse?
8. Do you sometimes say, "I'm sorry"?
9. Do you allow your spouse to "lose it" every once in a while?
10. Do you pray for each other regularly?
11. Do you show your love even when you don't feel like it?
12. Do you have eyes only for your partner?
13. Do you share your dreams and talk about how you can make them come true?
14. Do you expect to love and cherish your spouse for "as long as you both shall live"?
15. Do you frequently say, "I love you"?

ALICE GRAY, DR. STEVE STEPHENS, JOHN VAN DIEST

# 12 RULES FOR A HAPPY MARRIAGE

1. Never both be angry at once.
2. Never yell at each other unless the house is on fire.
3. Yield to the wishes of the other as an exercise in self-discipline if you can't think of a better reason.
4. If you have a choice between making yourself or your mate look good, choose your mate.
5. If you must criticize, do so lovingly.
6. Never bring up a mistake of the past. Your silence will be greatly appreciated.
7. Neglect the whole world rather than each other.
8. Never let the day end without saying at least one complimentary thing to your life's partner.
9. Never meet without an affectionate greeting.
10. When you've said or done something hurtful, acknowledge it and ask for forgiveness.
11. Remember, it takes two to get an argument going. Invariably the one who is wrong is the one who will be doing most of the talking.
12. Never go to bed mad.

ANN LANDERS
SYNDICATED COLUMNIST

# LITTLE THINGS FOR WIVES TO DO

- Pray for your husband daily.
- Show him you love him unconditionally.
- Tell him you think he's the greatest.
- Show him you believe in him.
- Don't talk negatively to him or about him.
- Tell him daily that you love him.
- Give him adoring looks.
- Show him that you enjoy being with him.
- Listen to him when he talks with you.
- Hug him often.
- Kiss him tenderly and romantically at times.
- Show him that you enjoy the thought of sex.
- Show him you enjoy meeting his sexual needs.
- Take the sexual initiative at times.
- Fix his favorite meal at an unexpected time.

- Demonstrate your dedication to him in public.
- Do things for him that he doesn't expect.
- Show others you are proud to be his wife.
- Rub his back, legs, and feet.
- Stress his strengths, not his weaknesses.
- Don't try to mold him into someone else.
- Revel in his joys; share his disappointments.
- Show him your favorite times are with him.
- Show him you respect him more than anyone else.
- Don't give him reason to doubt your love.
- Leave "I love you" notes in unexpected places.
- Give him your undivided attention often.
- Tell him he is your "greatest claim to fame."
- Let him hear you thank God for him.

KERBY ANDERSON
FROM "MARRIAGE, FAMILY, AND SEXUALITY"

# LITTLE THINGS FOR HUSBANDS TO DO

- Say "I love you" several times a day.
- Tell her often that she is beautiful.
- Kiss her several times a day.
- Hug her several times a day.
- Put your arm around her often.
- Hold her hand while walking.
- Come up behind her and hug her.
- Always sit by her when possible.
- Rub her feet occasionally.
- Give her a massage occasionally.
- Always open doors for her.
- Always help her with her chair.
- Ask her opinion when making decisions.
- Show interest in what she does.
- Take flowers to her unexpectedly.

- Plan a surprise night out.
- Ask if there are things you can do for her.
- Communicate with her sexually.
- Show affection in public places.
- Serve her breakfast in bed.
- Train yourself to think of her first.
- Show her you are proud to be her husband.
- Train yourself to be romantic.
- Write a love note on the bathroom mirror.
- Call during the day to say "I love you."
- Always call and tell her if you will be late.
- Let her catch you staring lovingly at her.
- Tell her she is your "greatest claim to fame."
- Let her hear you thank God for her.

KERBY ANDERSON
FROM "MARRIAGE, FAMILY, AND SEXUALITY"

# SEVEN COMMITMENTS FOR A STRONG MARRIAGE

1. COMMITMENT TO *oneness in body, spirit, and soul*
2. COMMITMENT TO *positive communication*
3. COMMITMENT TO *quality time together*
4. COMMITMENT TO *growth and improvement of the relationship*
5. COMMITMENT TO *emotional and sexual faithfulness*
6. COMMITMENT TO *honesty*
7. COMMITMENT TO *a lifelong love*

DR. STEVE STEPHENS
PSYCHOLOGIST AND SEMINAR SPEAKER

# REMEMBER TO LISTEN

*Listen*...and look each other in the eye as you share
and talk together.

*Listen*...and seek above all else to understand your mate.

*Listen*...and don't retreat when it feels uncomfortable.
Share what's really important.

*Listen*...and try not to defend yourself.
Remember, "winning" is not the goal; understanding is.

*Listen*...and don't react negatively to your mate's answers.
Instead, encourage each other to share
deeper feelings by asking more questions.

DENNIS AND BARBARA RAINEY
QUOTED FROM "TWO HEARTS ARE BETTER THAN ONE"

# HOW WELL DO WE COMMUNICATE?

1.
Both of us are available to listen when one of us wants to talk.

2.
Both of us are sympathetic and understanding when either of us wants to share deeper feelings.

3.
Neither of us has to weigh our words carefully to keep the other from getting angry or upset.

4.
Both of us usually have interesting things to talk about with each other.

5.
Both of us are generally satisfied with our efforts to please one another sexually, including open conversation about sex.

6.
Both of us see our partner as our best friend and feel free to share our hurts and frustrations, even when we don't agree.

7.
Both of us generally do not interrupt each other.

8.
Both of us make special efforts not to belittle
or put each other down in front of other people.

9.
Neither of us has a habit of criticizing or correcting the other.

10.
Both of us help the other feel good about him- or herself and let
the other know how valuable and important he or she is.

11.
Both of us understand and respect each other's desire
for occasional privacy and time to be alone.

12.
Neither of us hesitates to apologize when
we have offended the other.

13.
Both of us find ease in discussing our spiritual life together.

14.
Both of us are sensitive to the emotional
support we both desire and need.

FLORENCE AND FRED LITTAUER
ADAPTED FROM "AFTER EVERY WEDDING COMES A MARRIAGE"

# WHAT IF...

*...she really didn't mean to say those hurtful words?*

*...he honestly forgot your birthday?*

*...the grass isn't greener on the other side of the condominium complex?*

*...your problems don't last forever?*

*...you're both wrong?*

*...you discover that the kids aren't better off without you?*

*...you're throwing away something that's irreplaceable?*

*...you can never get it back?*

*...you didn't leave?*

*...you gave it one more chance?*

*...you fell in love all over again?*

*...this time things truly were different?*

*...you made it?*

MARTHA BOLTON
CONDENSED FROM "STILL THE ONE"

# 10 REASONS WHY DIVORCE ISN'T THE ANSWER

1.
It rarely solves the problem.

2.
It is a financial disaster.

3.
It blocks personal growth and maturity.

4.
It sets you both up to repeat your difficulty with someone else.

5.
It hardens your heart.

6.
It weakens your faith.

7.
It increases your loneliness.

8.
It devastates your children.

9.
It hurts friends and relatives.

10.
It impacts your legacy.

DR. STEVE STEPHENS
PSYCHOLOGIST AND SEMINAR SPEAKER

# SEVEN STEPS TO PREVENT DIVORCE

1.

**Make a commitment to stay together and to be faithful.**

When you determine to stay together and be faithful to each other, you are less likely to drift into thinking, *Maybe separation or unfaithfulness would be better than what we've got now.*

2.

**Pray and worship.**

Families that pray together do stay together—that's more than a slogan. Likewise, those who worship together regularly are often more happily married than those who don't.

3.

**Communicate, even when you don't feel like it —especially when you don't feel like it.**

Communication involves taking the time to listen, even when taking time is not convenient.

4.

**Practice forgiveness.**

A good marriage has been described as the union of two "awfully good forgivers."

5.

**Help one another, and bear each other's burdens.**

Marriage is a partnership, and good partners help each other. Whatever you think, be ready to lend a helping hand when your spouse needs it, even if that normally isn't your job!

6.

**Take time away.**

We all need time to get away from the pressures of life. Sometimes couples need rest and rejuvenating time together, away from the kids.

7.

**Fight the tendency to drift apart.**

Couples often drift apart without anybody noticing. We get busy with our individual activities and forget to keep our spouses involved.

GARY C. COLLINS
CONDENSED FROM "FAMILY SHOCK"

# HOW TO BE HAPPY IN MARRIAGE

*If you will be happy in marriage…*

CONFIDE

LOVE

BE PATIENT

BE FAITHFUL

BE FIRM

BE HOLY

MARTIN F. TUPPER
NINETEENTH-CENTURY WRITER

# MARITAL DATING

1. Make dating a top priority.
2. Ask your spouse out formally.
3. Set up regular date nights.
4. Alternate who plans the dates. (She plans one, then he plans one, then it's her turn again.)
5. Be positive if your partner chooses a place that isn't your favorite. (Remember that it's who you're with, not what you do, that's important.)
6. Be creative, and don't get in the rut of doing the same old thing.
7. Make sure you spend some time during the date talking and listening.
8. Don't talk about finances, children, or problems on a date.
9. Be on your very best behavior.
10. Do something romantic.
11. Hold hands.
12. Have fun.

ALICE GRAY, DR. STEVE STEPHENS, JOHN VAN DIEST

# QUESTIONS FOR SHARING YOUR DREAMS AND HOPES

- If we became richer than either of us could imagine today, what would you like to do with the money?

- What dreams have you followed? What dreams have you thrown away or kept secret?

- Of all the gifts you've received, which do you cherish most? Of all the gifts you've given, which did you enjoy giving the most?

- If you knew you had just six more months to live, how would you spend them? What would you do? Where would you go?

- In what three specific ways could we improve our everyday communication? Where are we strong in our communication? Where do we hit snags?

- What two or three problems if solved would make the most positive difference in our marriage and family?

- What do you think have been the most romantic times we've had together? How can we keep the romantic side of our marriage alive and exciting?

- What are the five most important milestones we've passed together? Why was each so important to you?

- If you could keep only one memory (of some past event or period of time), what would it be? Why?

- If our house caught on fire (and everyone was safely out), what three things would you most want to save? Why?

DENNIS AND BARBARA RAINEY
SELECTED FROM "TWO HEARTS ARE BETTER THAN ONE"

# FAITH AFFIRMATIONS FOR A WIFE

*I will stand beside my husband.*

*I will be trustworthy.*

*I will enrich his life.*

*I will appreciate him and all he does.*

*I will take care of his needs.*

*I will yearn deeply for him.*

*I will share my body with him.*

*I will cooperate and work with him.*

*I will love and respect him.*

*I will hate divorce.*

SELECTED FROM "THE HOLY BIBLE"

# FAITH AFFIRMATIONS FOR A HUSBAND

- I will hold my wife close to my heart.
- I will protect her.
- I will praise her publicly.
- I will compliment her.
- I will trust and treasure her.
- I will listen to her.
- I will always be faithful.
- I will never abuse or abandon her.
- I will love her night and day.
- I will grow old with her.

SELECTED FROM "THE HOLY BIBLE"

# GIFTS FOR YOUR SPOUSE

1. **The Gift of Sharing:**
   Talking about my hopes and fears and all that is in my heart.

2. **The Gift of Friendship:**
   Being the best friend I can be.

3. **The Gift of Time:**
   Encouraging you to spend time doing what you enjoy most.

4. **The Gift of Commitment:**
   Standing beside you through thick and thin, sickness and health, good times and bad.

5. **The Gift of Attention:**
   Listening to what you say and taking it seriously.

6. **The Gift of Respect:**
   Treating you with courtesy in both word and deed.

7. **The Gift of Humility:**
   Admitting that I am not always right and being willing to change where needed.

8. **The Gift of Encouragement:**
   Looking for opportunities to compliment you and build you up.

9. **The Gift of Care:**
   Doing my best to know and meet your emotional needs.

10. **The Gift of Forgiveness:**
    Forgiving you, getting over it, and not bringing it up again.

11. **The Gift of Generosity:**
    Showing you my love by giving time, words, tangible things, and memories.

12. **The Gift of Honesty:**
    Being totally open and honest and not keeping secrets.

13. **The Gift of Laughter:**
    Playing and having fun together.

14. **The Gift of Dreams:**
    Planning the future together with the commitment that we will spend the rest of our days side by side.

DR. STEVE STEPHENS
PSYCHOLOGIST AND SEMINAR SPEAKER

# CONTENTMENT

*Finding peace and fulfillment*

6

# SYMPHONY OF CONTENTMENT

TO LIVE CONTENT with small means,

TO SEEK ELEGANCE rather than luxury, and refinement rather than fashion,

TO BE WORTHY, not respectable, and wealthy, not rich,

TO STUDY HARD, think quietly, talk gently, act frankly,

TO LISTEN TO STARS and birds, to babes and sages, with open heart,

TO BEAR ALL cheerfully, do all bravely, await occasions, hurry never,

IN A WORD to let the spiritual, unbidden and unconscious, grow up through the common,

*This is to be my symphony.*

WILLIAM HENRY CHANNING
CHAPLAIN DURING THE CIVIL WAR

# 15 WAYS TO CHEER YOURSELF UP

- Pat yourself on the back for all the many things you have done right in your life.
- Listen closely to the advice of loved ones.
- Ask everyone you know to tell you stories about miracles in their lives.
- Attend a benefit for a worthy cause.
- Reread your favorite childhood book before you drift off to sleep.
- Learn to laugh at yourself.
- Make definite plans for your immediate future.
- Say grace before each meal.
- Practice looking on the bright side of life.
- Make someone else feel valuable.
- Try to be happy about others' good fortune.
- Learn to accept compliments.
- Go somewhere you have never been.
- Do what you loved to do as a child.
- Let go of regrets.

CYNDI HAYNES
CONDENSED FROM "2002 WAYS TO CHEER YOURSELF UP"

# KEEPING JOY IN YOUR LIFE

- *Keep something green* in a little vase or pot over your kitchen sink.

- *Find a small gift book that lifts your spirits and gives you hope*—prayers, affirmations, Scripture verses, or even just pretty pictures.

- *Schedule a lunch break or an afternoon tea* out with an encouraging friend.

- *Spend an occasional lunch hour rocking newborns* in a hospital nursery or volunteering at a day-care center.

- *Find a lovely place where you can walk to boost your spirits*—a park, an arboretum, a beautifully landscaped mall. Try to walk there at least once a week.

- *Put together a collection of things that mean hope to you*—pictures of your family, pebbles from a beach, a hank of kite string, a tulip bulb, or a miniature cross.

EMILIE BARNES
CONDENSED FROM "A CUP OF HOPE"

# ONLY THREE THINGS YOU NEED

A garden

A library

And someone to share them with.[1]

MARCUS TULLIUS CICERO, STATESMAN, PHILOSOPHER, AND ORATOR

1. THIS LINE ADDED BY EDITORS.

# THREE GOALS FOR MY LIFE

1.
To understand myself

2.
To see what God really wishes me to do

3.
To find the idea for which I can live and die

SOREN KIERKEGAARD
PHILOSOPHER AND THEOLOGIAN

# 18 WAYS TO FEEL BETTER

1.
Call a friend.

2.
Drive to the supermarket and buy fresh flowers
for your kitchen table.

3.
Give someone a compliment.

4.
Eat five bites of something rich and fattening and delicious.

5.
Put on your favorite CD and dance.

6.
Sit on the porch, and drink tea from your most elegant china.

7.
Do one thing you've been putting off for months.

8.
Plant something.

9.
Take a minivacation.

10.
Rekindle your dreams.

11.
Simplify your life.

12.
Protect your privacy.

13.
Forgive someone who hurt you.

14.
Guard your thoughts.

15.
Take care of your body.

16.
Tend to your soul.

17.
Write in your journal.

18.
Pray for your friends and family.

KAREN SCALF LINAMEN
CONDENSED FROM "SOMETIMES I WAKE UP GRUMPY...AND SOMETIMES I LET HIM SLEEP"

# HOW TO BE HAPPIER EVERY DAY

1.
Make a contract with yourself to stay focused on the upbeat.

2.
Constantly check to see if your attitude is worth catching.

3.
Always have something to look forward to.

JOAN LUNDEN
FROM "WAKE-UP CALLS," AS QUOTED IN "FAMILY CIRCLE" MAGAZINE

# ESSENTIALS FOR HAPPINESS

*Something* TO DO

*Something* TO LOVE

*Something* TO HOPE FOR

JOSEPH ADDISON
POET AND ESSAYIST

# LESS IS MORE

**Relationships**

Every additional person with whom you try to connect takes energy from others you care about. Make deliberate choices. You don't have to be best friends with the whole congregation at church or everyone on your block. Surface relationships are okay—if based on respect and kindness.

**Communication**

Every word you say uses energy. Keep opinions, criticisms, and information at a minimum. Try to joke, listen, compliment, and smile more.

**Information**

In today's cyber age, you could spend every waking moment taking in information. What could you do with the thirty minutes you normally spend watching the news? What if you tossed mail from solicitors unopened? Even coupon-cutting isn't always worth its value in time lost.

**Responsibility**

"But if I don't do it, then no one will!" Yes, shirking responsibilities can have consequences. But occasionally the consequences are preferable. Let the vacuuming go for a few days and see if anyone is any worse for the wear.

**Sensitivity**

Love is the greatest gift you have to offer. Make it a priority. However, don't be responsible for the results. If you give love and your recipient is still sour-faced, remember that he was already that way.

KAREN HAYSE
CONDENSED FROM WWW.MAXEDOUT.NET

# UNDERSTANDING CONTENTMENT

*Contentment makes poor men rich;*
*discontentment makes rich men poor.*
BENJAMIN FRANKLIN

*He who is not concerned with what he has*
*would not be content with what he would like to have.*
SOCRATES

*Make the most of the best and the least of the worst.*
ROBERT LOUIS STEVENSON

*I am always content with what has happened,*
*for I know that what God chooses is better than what I choose.*
EPICTETUS

# SLOW DOWN AND...

...walk in something soft with bare feet.

...touch a face with your eyes closed.

...watch the wind.

...feel your breath in your nostrils as you inhale and exhale.

...eat slowly and taste your food.

...feel your heart while you smile.

...smell flowers.

...listen to water.

...watch the moon rise.

...touch a baby.

LEE L. JAMPOLSKY
FROM "SMILE FOR NO GOOD REASON"

# POSITIVE PRINCIPLES

1\.
Being positive originates in a peaceful mind.

2\.
The power of being positive is
articulated through a pleasant mouth.

3\.
The power of being positive circulates by positive methods.

4\.
The power of being positive disintegrates personal misery.

5\.
Positive thinking is powerful medicine.

MIKE HUCKABEE, GOVERNOR OF ARKANSAS
CONDENSED FROM "LIVING BEYOND YOUR LIFETIME"

# APPRECIATING GOOD DAYS

- *Give thanks, over and over again.* Recognize the rarity and beauty of the gift. Appreciate it. Store the moments in your memory.

- *Share the day with someone you love*—either by doing something together or by telling somebody about it.

- *Capture the good day for the future* by writing in your journal, sketching the beauty around you, talking about it to your children.

- *When the day is over, let it go with good grace.* Smile and sigh and trust God for tomorrow.

EMILIE BARNES
FROM "A CUP OF HOPE"

# HOW TO BE REALLY CONTENT

- TAKE THE FOCUS OFF YOURSELF.
  As long as you think about your personal contentment, it will elude you.

- LIVE FREE OF DEBT.
  Financial and emotional debt keep you trapped in the past.

- SPEND SOME TIME ALONE.
  You need quiet time away from the hectic activities and noise of life so you can find the peace of mind that comes with internal silence.

- DO SOMETHING SPECIAL FOR SOMEONE WHO IS OLDER.
  Respect for and generosity toward those with more life experience bring great satisfaction.

- KEEP YOUNG CHILDREN IN YOUR LIFE.
  Children can teach you much about innocence, hope, joy, and simplicity.

- GET INVOLVED IN A WORTHWHILE CAUSE.
  When you volunteer for something bigger than you, you realize that you really can make a difference.

- AVOID NEGATIVE PEOPLE.
  Negative people can steal contentment from the best of situations.

- DISCIPLINE YOURSELF.
  Self-discipline gives you freedom. It helps you accomplish and enjoy those things that are truly important to you.

- UNDERSTAND THE OTHER PERSON'S POINT OF VIEW.
  This will dissipate negative and energy-wasting emotional responses. It can also give you compassion, sensitivity, and sometimes even wisdom.

- TREAT YOURSELF.
  Occasionally it's nice to relax and remind yourself that you are a person of value and worth.

- BE THANKFUL FOR WHAT YOU HAVE.
  The pursuit of pleasure is short-lived and never brings long-term satisfaction.

- ASK FOR ADVICE.
  There is much you do not know, and seeking wisdom and/or direction from those around you can bring joys you never expected.

- AVOID KNOWN TEMPTATIONS.
  There are things in life that seem attractive, but they are actually dangerous and destructive. Flee them.

KAREN L. WILLOUGHBY
EDITOR AND WRITING COACH

# EIGHT PROVEN STEPS TOWARD FEELING GOOD

1.
Learn to accept change.

2.
Admit your weaknesses.

3.
Ask for any help that you know you need.

4.
Be open to solutions.

5.
Deal directly with your problems.

6.
Admit your faults.

7.
Take full responsibility for your heart.

8.
Tell the truth, especially to yourself.

CYNDI HAYNES
FROM "2002 WAYS TO CHEER YOURSELF UP"

# LIFE

*Growing through the passages of time*

# 7

IF I COULD LIVE LIFE ALL OVER AGAIN...

TAMING FEARS

MENDING A BROKEN HEART

UNDERSTANDING FAITH

FOUR QUALITIES OF HARDY PEOPLE

SURVIVING BAD DAYS

THINGS I WISH I KNEW WHEN I WAS YOUNGER

SECRETS TO LIVING BEYOND 90

WHY OLDER IS BETTER

10 COMMANDMENTS FOR A SUCCESSFUL RETIREMENT

ACTIVITIES FOR A GREAT RETIREMENT

MYTHS ABOUT AGING

MYTHS ABOUT GRIEF

GIFTS TO GIVE YOURSELF DURING BEREAVEMENT

HOW TO HELP ME AS I GRIEVE

LETTING GO

FIVE LESSONS FOR LIFE

50 GREAT GOALS FOR THE NEW YEAR

# IF I COULD LIVE LIFE ALL OVER AGAIN...

I'd relax.

I'd dare to make more mistakes next time.

I would take fewer things seriously and more things sillily.

I would climb more mountains and swim more rivers.

I'd perhaps have more real problems but fewer imaginary ones.

I would eat more ice cream and less meat and beans.

I would travel a lot lighter next time.

I would go to more dances.

I would pick more daisies.

TIM AND JULIE CLINTON
FROM "THE MARRIAGE YOU'VE ALWAYS WANTED"

# TAMING FEARS

1. SAY THE WORDS.

Outwit denial by verbalizing the truth.

2. RESEARCH THE OPTIONS.

Information has never been so readily available! Make some phone calls; search the Internet; read some literature; talk to someone in the know.

3. RALLY SUPPORT.

Rally a network of living, breathing human beings who can encourage you from this point on.

4. MAKE A PLAN.

Now finalize your plan of action. What exactly must you do to experience complete freedom from whatever it is you've been too afraid to admit to anyone, even yourself?

5. TAKE ACTION.

It takes time to make permanent changes in your life, so get started! In fact, it takes twenty-one days of practicing a new behavior before it starts to turn into a habit, so don't become discouraged if you can't solve your dilemma overnight.

KAREN SCALF LINAMEN
CONDENSED FROM "SOMETIMES I WAKE UP GRUMPY...AND SOMETIMES I LET HIM SLEEP"

# MENDING A BROKEN HEART

1. Honestly accept and acknowledge the wound.
2. Create a safe, loving, self-nurturing environment for healing.
3. Dare to do the hard work of getting better.
4. Affirm small steps and remember that healing takes time.
5. Keep it simple.
6. Get rid of old messages and critical self-talk.
7. Take care of yourself.
8. Grieve what needs to be grieved.
9. Don't be afraid to ask for help.
10. Laugh and do something fun every single day.
11. Quiet your heart, mind, spirit, and soul before your Creator.
12. Expand and enlarge your horizons.
13. Risk getting hurt again.
14. Live life to the fullest with as much zest as you can muster.

MARTY WILLIAMS
PASTOR OF FAMILY MINISTRIES

# UNDERSTANDING FAITH

*You will never learn faith in comfortable surroundings.*
A. B. SIMPSON

*Faith does not wait until it understands;*
*in that case it would not be faith.*
VANCE HAVNER

*Faith is saying "Amen" to God.*
MERV ROSELL

*A simple childlike faith…solves all the problems that come to us.*
HELEN KELLER

*The only way to learn strong faith is to endure strong trials.*
GEORGE MUELLER

*All work that is worth anything is done in faith.*
ALBERT SCHWEITZER

*Faith is not belief without proof, but trust without reservation.*
D. ELTON TRUEBLOOD

*Faith never knows where it is being led,*
*but it loves and knows the one who is leading.*
OSWALD CHAMBERS

*Faith is knowing there is an ocean because you have seen a brook.*
WILLIAM A. WARD

*Faith is the conviction of realities I cannot see or feel.*
PAMELA REEVE

*Faith is to believe what you do not yet see;*
*the reward for this faith is to see what you believe.*
SAINT AUGUSTINE

*Faith is the highest passion in a human being.*
SOREN KIERKEGAARD

*Faith leads us beyond ourselves. It leads us directly to God.*
POPE JOHN PAUL II

# FOUR QUALITIES OF HARDY PEOPLE

1. **Hardy people become powerful.**
   They ask what action they can take to get them to their goal. They spend little time assigning blame. They waste no energy in accusation.

2. **Hardy people control their attitude.**
   They put the difficulty in perspective and ask what choices they have.

3. **Hardy people meet challenges head on.**
   Instead of looking at a challenge as a calamity, they describe a challenge as an opportunity, a chance to learn something they otherwise might never have known.

4. **Hardy people are triumphant.**
   Challenge is an invitation, not a summons. It is a chance to deepen wisdom and expand inventiveness. Each triumph is one more important step taken toward a goal.

JANE KIRKPATRICK
ADAPTED FROM "A BURDEN SHARED"

# SURVIVING BAD DAYS

- Remind yourself that no matter what happens, twenty-four hours from now this day will be over!

- Gripe a little bit to someone who cares—because the support and prayers of someone who knows what you're going through can make all the difference.

- Count to ten before you respond to anyone. On bad days, your reactions tend to be off, and you could easily say something hurtful.

- Pay a little extra attention to caring for yourself on days when everything seems to go wrong. Try to get some exercise, to eat nutritious foods, to take your vitamins. And ask for help if you need it.

- Ask yourself, "Does God have something for me to learn on this terrible, horrible, no good, very bad day?"

EMILIE BARNES
CONDENSED FROM "A CUP OF HOPE"

# THINGS I WISH I KNEW WHEN I WAS YOUNGER

1.
Start exercising now.

2.
Use sunscreen.

3.
Believe that there's joy in getting older.

4.
Keep your sunny side up.

5.
Be money smart.

6.
Dare to make your dreams come true.

7.
Believe that you can make an impact.

8.
Take photos, tuck away keepsakes.

9.
Relish each moment.

LAURA MANSKE
CONDENSED FROM "MCCALL'S" MAGAZINE

# SECRETS TO LIVING BEYOND 90

- Work hard (but not too hard).
- Keep socially active.
- Live one day at a time.
- Eat your fruits and vegetables.
- Enjoy nature.
- Take naps.
- Read your Bible often.
- Keep quiet and stay out of other people's business.
- Tend a garden.
- Dance.
- Don't overeat.
- Volunteer to help those in need.
- Think positively.
- Have something to look forward to.
- Play bingo.

COLLECTED FROM INDIVIDUALS OVER NINETY YEARS OLD

# WHY OLDER IS BETTER

1. You appreciate one day at a time.
2. More people open doors for you.
3. You don't have to prove yourself.
4. The simple pleasures seem so much more valuable.
5. It's okay to forget.
6. You can go at your own pace.
7. You have more stories to tell.
8. There's nothing left to learn the hard way.
9. You have time to volunteer.
10. You get to be a grandparent.
11. You get senior discounts.
12. You've seen it all before, even if you don't remember where.
13. You can stay up as long as you want.
14. You discover the value of the things that have been around a while—old friends, old books, old memories, old songs, and old wine.
15. You finally have perspective.
16. Things take longer, but you have more time to do them.
17. You have a better chance of shooting your age with your golf score.

18. You have seen so many prayers answered.
19. You know that being kind is often more important than being right.
20. You finally have the time to start a new hobby or read a new book.
21. You have learned that people are much more important than things.
22. You don't have to worry about what to do when you grow up.
23. You know how important it is to count your blessings.
24. You can take as many naps as you'd like.
25. Heaven is closer.
26. You have real wisdom to share.
27. You realize that time is a treasure.
28. You have learned that great memories come from both hard times and good times.
29. It's the perfect time for looking inward, outward, forward, and upward.
30. You finally realize that what you can't see lasts longer than what you can.

COLLECTED FROM INDIVIDUALS OVER FIFTY YEARS OLD

# 10 COMMANDMENTS FOR A SUCCESSFUL RETIREMENT

I. BE ACTIVE.

Mind, body, and spirit are meant to be used. Like muscles, they grow and expand when used and waste away when not used.

II. EXERCISE REGULARLY.

The body slows down and atrophies when it is not used. Doctors agree that regular exercise promotes both mental and physical health.

III. LIVE YOUR FAITH.

You can speak to God every day and hear what His words are for you—words of love and mercy. Get a good daily devotional book and use it along with your favorite study Bible. Attend worship services regularly.

IV. HELP OTHERS.

The joy and satisfaction you get from helping others is great medicine for your soul. Retirement is a time to give something back to your community and to invest time in volunteer activities.

V. CONTROL YOUR WEIGHT.

Excess weight saps energy, corrodes your feelings about yourself, and overtaxes a number of body systems. A little discipline in this area goes a long way toward increasing the enjoyment of retirement.

VI. HAVE ANNUAL PHYSICALS.

Most serious health problems can be detected during annual physical exams. Nearly all of them that are detected early can be overcome. There is no better insurance for good health than regular physical exams.

VII. AVOID ACCIDENTS.

Accidents that would simply harm a younger person can debilitate or even kill a senior citizen.

VIII. BE COMPUTER LITERATE.

In the information age, no device opens the world of knowledge the way the computer does. Don't be afraid—computers can be easy to use and can add meaning and joy to your life.

IX. ENJOY HUMOR AND GOOD MUSIC.

There is a reason comedians and musicians have longer life spans than people in other occupations. Laughter and good music are like medicine to the body and spirit.

X. OBEY GOD'S TEN COMMANDMENTS.

These apply as much in the golden years as in childhood. Ask God's help to follow His commands.

L. JAMES AND JACKIE HARVEY
CONDENSED FROM "EVERY DAY IS SATURDAY"

# ACTIVITIES FOR A GREAT RETIREMENT

- *Education.* Early in life, schooling involves acquiring skills, so maybe you've never had the opportunity to study something just for the sheer joy of learning. Take classes at the local community college on a topic you want to know more about.

- *Outdoor activities.* Cooped up in an office, factory, or other building all day, you may have longed to spend more time outdoors. Turn your garden into the showplace you know it can be. Go fishing or take up bird-watching. Whatever your interest in the outdoors, enjoy it.

- *Hit the road.* Now you have the time to indulge your wanderlust. Make a list of the places you want to go, and make vacation-planning your hobby when you're not roaming.

- *Handwork.* Woodwork, needlework, and painting are just a few hands-on hobbies. To do them well takes time, something you had little of when you were working. Now you can perfect your craft. Make a place at home where you can work with your hands to your heart's content.

- *Speak out.* If an interest in politics and government has always played second fiddle to your career, give it first place now. Whether you run for office, work on someone else's campaign, or keep tabs on legislation that affects you, find a way to get involved.

- *Pet pleasure.* Perhaps you're someone who enjoys animals, and now that you have more time on your hands, you could provide a good home for a dog, cat, bird, or other pet. If you have the space and the desire, caring for a pet can be a rewarding experience. Pets can be loyal companions and have positive effects on your well-being.

CONDENSED FROM "ABOUT...ENJOYING RETIREMENT," A LIFE ADVICE® PAMPHLET
PUBLISHED BY METLIFE'S CONSUMER EDUCATION CENTER

# MYTHS ABOUT AGING

1\.
Aging is a boring subject.

2\.
All old people are pretty much the same.

3\.
An unsound body equals an unsound mind.

4\.
Memory is the first thing to go.

5\.
Use it or lose it.

6\.
Old dogs can't learn new tricks.

7\.
Old people are isolated and lonely.

8\.
Old people are depressed and have every right to be.

DOUGLAS H. POWELL
FROM "THE NINE MYTHS OF AGING: MAXIMIZING THE QUALITY OF LATER LIFE"

# MYTHS ABOUT GRIEF

1. Grief is a bad thing.
2. All people grieve in the same way.
3. You should not be angry about a loss.
4. You should keep busy and try to think about only pleasant things.
5. Over time, you will get over the loss.
6. You must be strong and try to keep your feelings under control.
7. It is best not to focus on or talk about the loss.
8. When grief is resolved, it never comes up again.
9. Children grieve like adults.
10. If you have a strong faith, the grief will not be as intense.

DR. STEVE STEPHENS
PSYCHOLOGIST AND SEMINAR SPEAKER

# GIFTS TO GIVE YOURSELF DURING BEREAVEMENT

- *Time:* Time to be alone and time with people who are willing to listen when you want to talk. Time to pray, time to cry, and time to remember.
- *Rest:* Extra sleep, unhurried hot baths, naps.
- *Hope:* Being with others who have "survived" the death ordeal may offer you proof that you can heal.
- *Goals:* Make a list of goals for today and another list for the week. Unless necessary, don't plan very far ahead right now.
- *Goodness:* Take in a movie, eat a hot-fudge sundae with a friend, sit in a hot tub, or have a massage.
- *Permission to backslide:* Old feelings of sadness, despair, or anger may return. This is normal and should not be considered failure. Accept it as a "bad day" and remember, "This, too, shall pass."
- *A special friend:* It is important that you not attempt to handle grief alone. At some time you need to share your responses to grief with a good friend or someone who can listen objectively. If you become concerned about your progress over a period of six to nine months, don't hesitate to get some professional counseling.

BARBARA BAUMGARDNER
FROM "A PASSAGE THROUGH GRIEF"

# HOW TO HELP ME AS I GRIEVE

- Don't avoid me.
- Send me a card…even as time goes on.
- Understand that I need to be alone sometimes.
- Please don't give advice; it doesn't help.
- Make concrete offers to help with yard work, errands, etc.
- Coordinate with others to bring food I can eat.
- Don't take over for me. I need to do some things for myself.
- Give me time; don't expect too much too soon.
- Listen to the story of the loss…sometimes over and over.
- Don't be surprised if I do something unexpected.
- Understand that I may feel guilt or anger at times.
- Check in on me as time goes on.
- Remember my loved one with me.
- Don't try to fix me.
- Accept my silence.

PROVIDENCE HOME AND COMMUNITY SERVICES—COMMUNITY CARE PROJECT
PORTLAND, OREGON

# LETTING GO

LETTING GO *is not to stop caring—it means I can't do it for someone else.*

LETTING GO *is not to cut myself off—it's the realization that I can't control another.*

LETTING GO *is not to enable—but to allow learning from natural consequences.*

LETTING GO *is to admit powerlessness—which means the outcome is not in my hands.*

LETTING GO *is not to try to change or blame another—it's to make the most of myself.*

LETTING GO *is not to fix—but to be supportive; it's not to judge—but to allow another to be a human being.*

LETTING GO *is not to be in the middle, arranging the outcome—but to allow others to effect their own destinies.*

LETTING GO *is not to be protective—it's to permit another to face reality.*

LETTING GO *is not to deny—but to accept.*

LETTING GO *is not to nag, scold, or argue—but instead to search out my own shortcomings and correct them.*

LETTING GO *is not to criticize and regulate anybody—but to try to become what I dream I can be.*

LETTING GO *is not to regret the past—but to grow and live for the future.*

LETTING GO *is to fear less and live more.*

AUTHOR UNKNOWN

# FIVE LESSONS FOR LIFE

**Keep your word and your commitments.**

If you get married, stay married. Your children need stability, and marriage is not to be lightly shed like old clothes.

**Don't look for favors—count on earning them.**

Although so much is built on whom you know and not what you know, don't rely on whom you know. Those who give can also take away.

**Watch out for success—it can be more dangerous than failure.**

Don't park on yesterday's accomplishments and think you don't have to keep striving and stay vigilant.

**Do what you say, say what you mean, and be what you seem.**

Do not pretend to be what you are not or let other people define who and what you are. There is too much falsehood and pretense in politics, in business, in the religious community, and in the media.

**Open the envelope of your soul to discern God's orders hidden there.**

The Danish philosopher Kierkegaard believed that each of us is born with God's instructions inside, which we must struggle to understand and act upon.

MARIAN WRIGHT EDELMAN
CONDENSED FROM "PARADE" MAGAZINE

# 50 GREAT GOALS FOR THE NEW YEAR

1. Eat healthfully. 2. Exercise well. 3. Compliment friends. 4. Seek simplicity. 5. Reduce your vices. 6. Increase your virtues. 7. Worry less. 8. Buy less. 9. Read more. 10. Read the right stuff. 11. Watch more sunsets and less TV. 12. Listen to good music. 13. Spend time each day in solitude. 14. Meditate on who God really is. 15. Pray often. 16. Always speak the truth. 17. Show more love. 18. Listen to children. 19. Visit the elderly. 20. Take time for friends. 21. Follow the example of those you admire most. 22. Maintain a positive attitude. 23. Keep promises. 24. Laugh as often as possible. 25. Be kind to all you meet. 26. Forgive any who wrong you. 27. Apologize to those you might have wronged. 28. Encourage the discouraged. 29. Give generously to those in need. 30. Thank those who have given to you. 31. Work hard and play hard. 32. Clear the clutter from each day. 33. Seek the best in others. 34. Deepen your faith. 35. Truly look at, listen to, and feel all that surrounds you. 36. Appreciate the beauty of nature. 37. Try something new. 38. Greet more strangers. 39. Learn the art of patience. 40. Recall good memories and forget regrets. 41. Give more hugs. 42. Recognize possibilities instead of obstacles. 43. Right a wrong. 44. Help someone's dream come true. 45. Keep a journal. 46. Live a humble life. 47. Dwell on what is noble and praiseworthy. 48. Take more walks. 49. Hold more hands. 50. Build a legacy that is respected.

ALICE GRAY, DR. STEVE STEPHENS, JOHN VAN DIEST

# 8

# HOME AND FINANCES

*Managing your nest and your nest egg*

# PROPER MONEY MANAGEMENT

1.
Give some away.

2.
Keep some.

3.
It is better not to borrow;
but if you cannot avoid it, repay the debt quickly.

4.
Do not spend money that doesn't belong to you.

5.
Do not become preoccupied with money.

6.
Don't fall in love with money!

MARY HUNT
FROM "THE FINANCIALLY CONFIDENT WOMAN"

# HOW TO RECOGNIZE A RISKY INVESTMENT

1. Is the prospect of a large profit "practically guaranteed"?
2. Does the decision to invest need to be made quickly, allowing you no opportunity to thoroughly investigate the investment or the promoter?
3. Does the promoter say he has an "excellent track record" and is doing you a "favor" by allowing you to invest with him?
4. Does the investment offer attractive tax deductions as an incentive?
5. Do you know little or nothing about the particular investment?
6. Is very little said about the risks of losing money?
7. Does the investment appear to require no effort on your part?
8. Are you promised a "handsome profit" quickly?

HOWARD L. DAYTON JR.
FROM "GETTING OUT OF DEBT"

# WARNING SIGNS THAT YOU NEED FINANCIAL COUNSELING

- Do you pay only the minimum, or less, on your credit cards each month?
- Do you juggle other bills to keep up the minimum monthly payments on each credit card?
- Have you reached the credit limit on your credit cards?
- Do you use cash advances to pay monthly bills?
- Are you paying late fees?
- Are you getting letters and phone calls from angry creditors and collectors?
- Have you taken money from your savings account to pay your credit-card bills?
- Are you confused about which creditor to pay first?
- Are you plagued by a bad credit history or contemplating bankruptcy?

MARY MCLEAN HIX
CONDENSED FROM "HOMELIFE" MAGAZINE

# TEACHING KIDS TO HANDLE MONEY

1. *Earn diligently.*
   Earning money gives your child a sense of worth.

2. *Save consistently.*
   If your child learns to save something each time he gets some money, he has learned a valuable lesson that many in this generation have lost.

3. *Give cheerfully.*
   Early in life, children should learn the satisfaction of helping others.

4. *Spend wisely.*
   It's amazing how fast kids learn the difference between a wise investment and a waste of money when they're spending their own dollars.

5. *Receive graciously.*
   Our joy in giving is multiplied because we know the pleasure of receiving.

KEN CANFIELD
CONDENSED FROM "TODAY'S FATHER" MAGAZINE

# PRACTICAL LESSONS WITH MONEY

- Give your child five dollars to invest in something that will make more money. Arrange for him to repay you after a month; let him keep the profits.
- Ask your child what she would do with one hundred dollars or one million dollars.
- Help your kids set up a budget applicable to them.
- Take your kids on an imaginary shopping spree using catalogs or the Internet. Give them a budget and some general buying objectives.
- Take the kids to garage sales. Give each child a dollar and watch how they spend it.
- Encourage your children to lay a portion of their money aside for church or another charity.
- Take a five- or ten-dollar bill and have the whole family think of ways to squeeze the most fun out of it.
- Buy your child ten shares of stock in a company that he will recognize, and watch the investment make or lose money.
- Teach your child to clip coupons and give him a percentage of the money you save.

KEN CANFIELD
CONDENSED FROM "TODAY'S FATHER" MAGAZINE

# 15 WAYS TO SPEND LESS MONEY

1. Stop trying to impress other people.
2. Stop shopping.
3. Purchase with cash.
4. Keep a spending record.
5. Save first, spend later.
6. Buy used if at all possible.
7. Buy, don't lease.
8. Increase your automobile insurance deductible.
9. Grocery shop with a list.
10. Arrive at the grocery store with cash only.
11. Stock up on sale items.
12. Avoid convenience food.
13. Don't bounce checks.
14. Use cold water in laundry.
15. Write postcards instead of calling long distance.

MARY HUNT
CONDENSED FROM "THE FINANCIALLY CONFIDENT WOMAN"

# FINANCIAL PERSPECTIVE

1. Realize that money can't make you happy.
2. Live for what really matters.
3. Know that riches will pass away.
4. Be content with what you have.
5. Put people above money.
6. Share what you have with the ones you love.
7. Invest in the right places.
8. Keep character above acquiring.
9. Don't cling to what you have.
10. Give generously to things that will last beyond your lifetime.

JOHN VAN DIEST
ASSOCIATE PUBLISHER

# 10 WAYS TO SAVE ON GASOLINE

1. **Keep starts and stops smooth.**
   Nailing the pedal to the floor in "jackrabbit starts" wastes gas. Abrupt stops also waste fuel—and cause extra wear and tear.

2. **Perform routine car care.**
   Change your oil and check the filters every three thousand miles for peak performance.

3. **Maintain tires and keep wheels aligned.**
   Low tire air pressure is dangerous—and costly. Misaligned wheels, worn wheel bearings, or dragging brakes also can reduce fuel economy by 10 percent.

4. **Buy the right octane.**
   Most cars work fine on regular gas. Use the octane the carmaker specifies.

5. **Use your air conditioner wisely.**
   Running your air conditioner greatly increases gas consumption. Don't use it if fresh air will cool the vehicle sufficiently.

6. **Lighten the load.**
   Don't use your trunk to store stuff. Added weight lowers fuel economy.

7. **Stay out of traffic.**
   Stop-and-go traffic takes a drastic toll on fuel usage. If at all possible, plan your trips to avoid periods of peak traffic congestion.

8. **Drive smart.**
   First, keep your speed down: Going sixty-five miles per hour uses about 15 percent more fuel than going fifty-five miles per hour, and going seventy to seventy-five miles per hour may consume 25 percent more. Second, keep a constant speed—use cruise control if you can.

9. **Plan your errands.**
   Try to combine errands with your daily commute: Pick up your dry cleaning on the way home from work, for example.

10. **Fill up in the morning.**
    You'll get slightly more fuel for your dollar if you fill up when it's cooler outside. (Cooler gasoline is more compact.)

BOB CERULLO
CONDENSED FROM "PARADE" MAGAZINE

# TRAVEL TIPS

*Before leaving home:*

- Give your relatives or friends your itinerary.
- Unplug small appliances.
- Have newspapers and mail stopped.
- Leave a key with a neighbor or relative so he or she can check the house while you're gone.
- Write down numbers of all credit cards you're taking along, with the addresses and toll-free U.S. phone numbers of the issuers so that you can notify them in case the cards are lost or stolen.
- Photocopy the information page of your passport. Carry a copy separately when you travel.
- Use the hotel's or ship's safe for credit cards and other valuables.
- Don't pack valuables in your check-in luggage; keep them with you.
- Carry all medications with you.

YVONNE BEEMAN
FROM "SENIOR LIFE" MAGAZINE

# LETTING GO OF THE FAMILY HOME

***Consider what you need in a new home.***

It's important to recognize the things about your old home that nourish you. Even if you're moving someplace smaller, try to re-create these characteristics so that living there will feel good to you.

***Hang on to the essentials.***

You may need to throw out or sell items that won't fit with your new lifestyle, but don't go overboard in the name of simplifying.

***Keep a mental accounting of what you're giving up and gaining.***

Yes, you may be losing a large basement or formal dining room, but do you really use them much?

***Don't confuse emotional and financial value.***

Accept that your fond memories of your old home do not necessarily add to its market value.

***Seek a sense of closure.***

Before the moving van comes, remind yourself of all that happened in your home. Go over it, experience the past, and have a good cry if you want to. A teary reaction is perfectly natural.

JUDITH D. SCHWARTZ
CONDENSED FROM "NEW CHOICES" MAGAZINE

# HOW TO DO (ALMOST) EVERYTHING

1.

LIST IT.

Divide your to-do list into three levels: "A" things yield the most value for your time. "B" activities are maybes. "C" items can wait.

2.

ANTICIPATE IT.

Hang a large calendar at a central location in your home and make sure all upcoming commitments get on this calendar.

3.

DELEGATE IT.

Get help. Delegate jobs to others and even to machines (such as Crock-Pots and answering machines).

4.

MULTI-TASK IT.

Be focused and do several things at the same time. Consolidate errands into one trip. Make the most of your time.

5.
SIMPLIFY IT.

Something done at 80 percent is better than something waiting to be started. Don't try to do a task perfectly; just try and get it done.

6.
ENERGIZE IT.

Know when that time of day is when you have the most energy and brainpower. Use that time for your most important tasks. Also, know that time of day when you most need to unwind. Use that to relax and reenergize.

JEANNE ZORNES
ADAPTED FROM "TODAY'S CHRISTIAN WOMAN" MAGAZINE

# DE-JUNKING YOUR HOME

## BOX 1
***Junk***

Into this box goes obvious trash and stuff so awful you don't want to sic it on anyone else, even if it's in perfect condition.

## BOX 2
***Charity***

It's still good and useful, but not for you—you don't want, need, or like it anymore. So put it in here and pass it along to a relative, friend, or the charity of your choice.

## BOX 3
***Sort***

It's something you still want or need, but it isn't doing you any good where it is now. Drop it in here so it can be put in position to actually be used.

## BOX 4
***Emotional withdrawal***

Into this box go things you know you should get rid of, but you can't quite bring yourself to do it.

DON ASLETT
FROM "HOW TO HANDLE 1,000 THINGS AT ONCE"

# FIVE WAYS TO KEEP YOUR HOME RUNNING SMOOTHLY

1.

Establish what *smoothly* means for you and your family. Create a clear plan and direction for your family.

2.

Have a spot for everything and try to keep everything in its spot.

3.

Plan your daily chores, projects, and cleaning so you can focus consistently.

4.

Pick up the mess at night. That way each morning is a fresh new day without yesterday's clutter.

5.

Your new day begins the night before. Complete as much as possible each night to ensure your new day starts smoothly (write a list of errands, prepare lunches, select clothes to wear).

JANE JARRELL
FROM "MOM MATTERS"

# 12 TIME-MANAGEMENT TIPS FOR YOUR HOME

1. Identify "time stealers" and minimize them.
2. Work ahead, not behind.
3. Keep a running to-do list and mark off the items done.
4. Make a few simple neatness rules that apply to every family member.
5. Clean up as you go and maintain the areas that are already cleaned.
6. Cook more than one meal at a time. Freeze portions for later use.
7. De-junk your living space systematically, one area at a time.
8. Teach your children to love orderliness.
9. Plan outfits to wear for the week, especially if you work outside the home.
10. Get up fifteen minutes earlier.
11. Turn the TV off!
12. Consider your time too valuable to waste. Say "no" nicely!

PAT ABERNATHY
FROM "TIME-MANAGEMENT SEMINAR" PAMPHLET

# WHAT EVERY FAMILY MEMBER NEEDS TO KNOW

When and how to call 911

How to contact neighbors or relatives in an emergency

How to exit in case of fire

Location and use of collapsible ladders for upper floors

Medical problems and allergies of all family members

Where emergency items are kept

How to turn off gas, water, electricity, and computer equipment

Symptoms of carbon monoxide poisoning

When to answer the door if you are alone

How to answer the phone if an adult is not present

Address and cross streets of residence

PAT VAN DIEST
REGISTERED NURSE

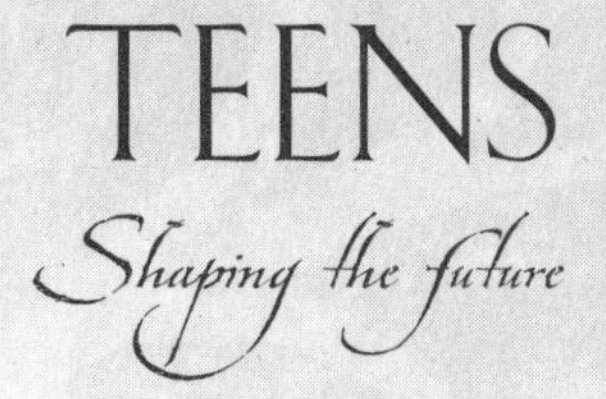


9

# EVERY TEEN STRUGGLES WITH...

1. ACHIEVEMENT—*the satisfaction of arriving at excellence in some endeavor.*

2. FRIENDS—*the broadening of one's social base by making friends and maintaining them.*

3. FEELINGS—*the self-understanding gained through sharing one's feelings with another person.*

4. IDENTITY—*the sense of knowing "who I am," of being recognized as a significant person.*

5. RESPONSIBILITY—*the confidence of knowing "I can stand alone and make responsible decisions."*

6. MATURITY—*the transformation from a child into an adult.*

7. SEXUALITY—*the acceptance of responsibility for one's new role as a sexual being.*

HOLMBECK, PAIKOFF, AND BROOKS-GUNN
FROM "HANDBOOK OF PARENTING: APPLIED AND PRACTICAL PARENTING"
AS PUBLISHED IN "FIVE CRIES OF PARENTS"

# FIVE ITEMS KIDS SAY THEY WANT

1.

*Good physical health*

2.

*One marriage partner for life*

3.

*A clear purpose in life*

4.

*Close, personal friendships*

5.

*A close relationship with God*

JOSH MCDOWELL
FROM "THE DISCONNECTED GENERATION"

# SIX CRITICAL PARENT-TEEN ISSUES

1.
*Curfew*

2.
*Cash*

3.
*Car*

4.
*Cohorts*

5.
*Conflict*

6.
*Consequences*

JOHN ROSEMOND
CONDENSED FROM "TEEN PROOFING"

# COMMON MISCONCEPTIONS ABOUT BUILDING SELF-ESTEEM

**Pitfall #1**

THE COMPLIMENTARY PARENT

***(focusing too much on your teen's looks)***

Although it's fine to tell your teenager she's attractive, to make her feel as if she is loved only because of her physical attributes is unhealthy.

**Pitfall #2**

THE JUDGMENTAL PARENT

***(focusing too much on others' bodies)***

Criticizing and judging others is rude and unnecessary, so why not keep unflattering thoughts to yourself?

**Pitfall #3**

THE SELF-CONSCIOUS PARENT

***(focusing too much on your own body)***

Finding peace with your body not only boosts your self-esteem; it helps your teen find peace with hers.

## Pitfall #4

THE DISCRIMINATORY PARENT

***(focusing too much on the differences between your daughter and son)***

Treat your children equally, and don't get sucked into gender traps concerning what's acceptable.

## Pitfall #5

THE DECISION-MAKING PARENT

***(focusing too much on your teenager's every choice)***

When your child is young and impressionable, guiding her to make healthy and safe choices is wise. However, once your child is a teenager, guiding her to think for herself and draw her own conclusions—particularly when she's old enough to think logically—is necessary to build healthy self-esteem.

CHRISTY HEITGER-CASBON
CONDENSED FROM "HOMELIFE" MAGAZINE

# HOW TO BUILD YOUR TEENAGER'S SELF-ESTEEM

1.

When you watch your teen in an athletic event, do you criticize the performance afterwards? Or do you talk about how proud you are to see the effort?

2.

When your teen brings home a school assignment, do you talk first about the questions that are wrong? Or do you immediately look for the ones that are right?

3.

When your teen needs helps with household chores, do you emphasize the thing that needs to be done better? Or do you give thanks for the help and talk about what was done especially well?

CHRISTY HEITGER-CASBON
CONDENSED FROM "HOMELIFE" MAGAZINE

# CONNECTING WITH TEENS

1.
AFFIRMATION
*giving youth a sense of authenticity*

2.
ACCEPTANCE
*giving youth a sense of security*

3.
APPRECIATION
*giving youth a sense of significance*

4.
AFFECTION
*giving youth a sense of lovability*

5.
AVAILABILITY
*giving youth a sense of importance*

6.
ACCOUNTABILITY
*giving youth a sense of responsibility*

JOSH MCDOWELL
ADAPTED FROM "THE DISCONNECTED GENERATION"

# ADULTS WHO ARE MOST SUCESSFUL WITH TEENS...

- provide clear and positive acceptance.
- encourage and reinforce honest communication.
- let teens know they're liked and that they "belong."
- are enthusiastic—no sticks-in-the-mud allowed.
- show up to make it happen.

WILLIAM J. BEAUSAY II
REPRINTED FROM "TEENAGE BOYS!"

# SIX PRINCIPLES OF INTENTIONAL PARENTING

*Don't just be there; be audaciously present.*

*Don't try to force change; provoke it.*

*Don't just have a good attitude; get a great metaphor.*

*Don't tolerate teens; get passionate about them.*

*Don't get a bigger hammer; get a better idea.*

*Have fun.*

WILLIAM J. BEAUSAY II
REPRINTED FROM "TEENAGE BOYS!"

# PREPARE YOUR TEEN FOR THE UNEXPECTED

A. ***Help your kids expect the unexpected.***
The advent of the unexpected is not the end of the world.

B. ***Portray the unexpected as an opportunity rather than a disaster.***
How you personally respond to the unexpected will have a powerful impact on how your kids respond.

C. ***Tell your kids how other people have met unexpected challenges and gotten through them.***
This dynamic characterizes every true hero. This is the power of stories—classic stories, stories about true sports heroes, stories about your parents, stories from your own experience.

D. ***Remind them to stick to the fundamentals of their game plan and not to panic.***
Stay steady, and they will come through.

RICKY BYRDSONG
CONDENSED FROM "COACHING YOUR KIDS IN THE GAME OF LIFE"

# RULES FOR PARENT-TEEN COMMUNICATION

- Remember that actions speak louder than words.
- Define what is important and ignore what isn't.
- Be as realistic as possible.
- Be clear and specific.
- Check out your assumptions.
- Recognize that it is all right for two people to view the same thing differently.
- Recognize that your family members know you well.
- Keep discussions from turning into arguments.
- Accept all feelings and try to understand them.
- Be considerate and respectful.
- Do not preach or lecture; ask questions instead.
- Do not use excuses.
- Do not nag, yell, or whine.
- Know when to use humor and when to be serious.
- Above all, listen.

DR. LES PARROTT III
FROM "HELPING THE STRUGGLING ADOLESCENT"

# DO'S AND DON'TS FOR BETTER CONVERSATIONS WITH TEENS

**Don't say,** *"I'm older and wiser."*
**Do say,** *"I disagree with you, but tell me why you think that."*

**Don't say,** *"Because I said so, that's why!"*
**Do say,** *"You know the rules, and I'm holding you to them."*

**Don't say,** *"Go figure it out for yourself."*
**Do say,** *"I'll try to explain it to you."*

**Don't say,** *"When I was your age, I…"*
**Do say,** *"I want to know how you see the situation."*

**Don't say,** *"You'll never amount to anything!"*
**Do say,** *"You can achieve anything you desire—if you want to badly enough."*

**Don't say,** *"You shouldn't feel like that!"*
**Do say,** *"Tell me why you feel that way."*

**Don't say,** *"I told you so!"*
**Do say,** *"We all make mistakes. The idea is to learn from them."*

**Don't say,** *"Why can't you be like your sister (brother)?"*
**Do say,** *"You and your sister (brother) each have your own talents, and I love both of you very much."*

**Don't say,** *"You're just like your father (mother)!"*
**Do say,** *"You are a unique individual!"*

**Don't say,** *"How could you do this to me?"*
**Do say,** *"You are responsible for your actions—how they affect others as well as yourself."*

DON GABOR
FROM "SPEAKING YOUR MIND IN 101 DIFFICULT SITUATIONS"

# WHAT TEENS LOOK FOR IN A JOB

1. A boss who understands teens and their world
2. A place that has either other teens working there or people they can relate to
3. A schedule that offers flexibility
4. Clearly defined expectations, such as a written job description
5. A position that challenges them to develop useful skills
6. A boss who realizes that school comes first
7. A workplace that pays on time and fairly
8. A company with a good reputation in the community and among other workers
9. A job that's safe and doesn't threaten their health, body, or sleep and that they are proud to work at and can talk about
10. Employees who would be a good influence on them

TIM SMITH
FROM "LIFE SKILLS FOR GUYS"

# HOW TO SPOT DEPRESSION IN TEENS

1. Has your child stopped enjoying nearly all activities?

2. Does your child appear sad, and does she constantly complain of being tired? Does she cry for long periods, but can't explain her tears?

3. Does your child become agitated or angry? Is he masking his depression with displays of anger?

4. Have you noticed a change in your child's eating habits or observed a significant weight loss or gain?

5. Are your worried about your child's sleeping habits? Does your child complain about sleepless nights? Or does he or she sleep excessively?

6. Is the child's thinking slow, confused, and indecisive?

7. Do the child's statements show feelings of worthlessness, excessive blame, or inappropriate guilt?

8. Does she talk about death and suicide, or has she attempted suicide? (If so, get immediate help.)

WESLEY SHARPE
FROM "HOMELIFE" MAGAZINE

# DEALING WITH A DATING TEEN

- LISTEN TO YOUR TEENAGER'S IDEAS ABOUT DATING. Sometimes your teen tries out other's ideas to see how they sound. Sometimes your teen tests your boundaries, especially if you aren't clear about where those boundaries are. Many times teens just want to have input into the decisions being made about their lives. Try to use your teen's suggestions in setting dating boundaries.

- BE CONSISTENT. Don't let other parents sway you from values that you hold important. Talk about these values.

- BE A ROLE MODEL. Show the same respect and appreciation to your spouse and to your teenager that you want your teenager to show to a date.

- BE FAIR. BE REASONABLE. Don't project your bad dating experiences or poor dating judgment on to your teenager. Treat your teenager with the level of responsibility and trust that he or she consistently demonstrates.

- BE CLEAR. State what you expect from your dating teenager. Don't assume anything.

- BE CONSCIOUS OF SAFETY. Share your fears with your teenagers without being an alarmist. Provide safety supports where available.

- ONCE A YEAR, MORE OFTEN AS YOUR TEEN MATURES, CREATE A DATING CONTRACT. State the points of the contract in positive terms ("I will...") when possible, rather than negative ("I will not..."). Make the contract between you and your teen specific and appropriate for your teen's maturity level.

ANN B. GANNON
CONDENSED FROM "HOMELIFE" MAGAZINE

# A TEENAGER'S 10 AGREEMENTS

1.

Dad and Mom run the show here. It's not a democracy. My vote counts (a lot), but Dad and Mom decide.

2.

I agree to keep Mom and Dad notified of where I am at all times and to ask in advance if permission is necessary.

3.

I agree to treat every member of my family, youngest to oldest, with the respect, manners, and thoughtfulness reserved for my most important company.

4.

Physical or verbal violence is not okay here—no roughness or out-of-control behavior, no swearing or obscene language, name-calling, or rudeness.

5.

Alcohol, drugs, or cigarettes are not allowed in this house or on the property.

6.

Sexual intercourse between unmarried persons is not allowed. Pornography in any form is not allowed.

7.

I agree to keep the following schedule: get home by _____ on weeknights, _____ on weekends; bed by _____ on school nights. Sneaking out is not okay.

8.

I agree to tell the truth.

9.

I agree to respect the property and privacy of others (asking before borrowing, knocking before entering).

10.

I agree that important things come first here: Homework comes before television or computer time; chores come before play; church involvement comes first on Sunday.

WILLIAM J. BEAUSAY II
FROM "TEENAGE BOYS!"

# DOES YOUR TEEN NEED PROFESSIONAL HELP?

- Is your teen silent for long periods and often withdrawn socially, having few friends?
- Is your teen considering dropping out or in danger of not completing high school? Failing classes?
- Is your teen obsessed with exercise and diet? Does your teen have an eating disorder?
- Does your teen practice any form of self-mutilation in the form of teeth marks, cuts, or burns? Does he wear homemade tattoos?
- Is your teen involved in any kind of illegal activity? Has he been arrested or in trouble with the law?
- Does your teen show an excessive fear of a particular family member, other relative, or family friend? Could she have been sexually abused and fears to talk about it?
- Does your teen have long periods of feeling worthless, helpless, guilty, or lethargic? Does he suffer from depression?
- Is your home life in chaos because of your teen? Is your well-being or performance at work suffering because of your teen's problems?
- Does your teen show a strong interest in the occult? Does he read about black magic, or is he involved in antireligious activities?

- Does your teen blow up with anger and get into fights a great deal? Has he been involved in vandalism? Is he a threat to someone's physical well-being?
- Are you concerned that your teen may be sexually promiscuous? Is he or she risking venereal disease or pregnancy?
- Does your teen report hearing voices that others do not hear? Does she hallucinate, or is she out of touch with reality?
- Is your teen having serious problems with sleep, such as insomnia, repeated wakefulness at night, frequent nightmares, or sleeping too much?
- Does your teen have morbid thoughts or talk about death a lot? Is she suicidal?
- Does your teen run with a peer group that violates the rights of others? Do you have reason to suspect that he is involved in illegal activities or destructive acts?
- Does your teen get drunk? Does he drive while drinking? Is your teen experimenting with drugs that can kill?
- Does your teen experience relatively brief periods of intense anxiety? Does she suffer from panic attacks?

DR. LES PARROTT III
FROM "HELPING THE STRUGGLING ADOLESCENT"

# WHEN IT'S TIME TO LET GO

## REMEMBER...

Your child is not the legitimate center of life
(he is profoundly instructive, satisfying,
and pleasurable, but temporary).

Transition is easier when the job
of child-rearing is done well.

An adult child is responsible for his own decisions—
you cannot make them for him.

HOWARD AND JEANNE HENDRICKS
CONDENSED FROM "KINDRED SPIRIT" MAGAZINE

# FAMILY LESSONS

10

*Learning and maturing together*

EVERY CHILD NEEDS...

WAYS TO BE A BETTER DAD

WAYS TO BE A BETTER MOM

PARENTING TIPS

HEALTHY FAMILIES...

12 THINGS KIDS WORRY ABOUT

HOW TO GET YOUR KIDS TO HELP AT HOME

FIVE WAYS TO TEACH YOUR CHILD THE ART OF SHARING

FIVE STEPS TO BETTER BEHAVIOR

FOUR TIPS TO AVOID CLEANUP CONFLICT

SEVEN PRINCIPLES OF DISCIPLINE

GOOD MANNERS WHEN MEETING OTHERS

10 WAYS TO ENCOURAGE SELF-RELIANT BEHAVIOR

10 TIPS TO TRIGGER TALKING

CHILD PROOFING AGAINST CHEAP THRILLS

THINGS KIDS HATE TO HEAR

HELPING YOUR CHILDREN GET TO SLEEP

EIGHT WAYS TO HELP YOUR CHILD GET GOOD GRADES

SEVEN IRREDUCIBLE NEEDS

10 WAYS TO RAISE CHILDREN THAT WILL USE DRUGS

# EVERY CHILD NEEDS...

At least one adult who is a positive role model.

To feel accepted.

Recognition.

A sense of belonging.

To feel safe and secure.

Some control over his or her environment.

Social interaction skills.

To accept responsibility for his or her behavior.

LEAH DAVIES
CONDENSED FROM WWW.KELLYBEAR.COM

# WAYS TO BE A BETTER DAD

LOVE YOUR CHILDREN'S MOTHER
It is a precious gift a father passes on to his children.

SPEND TIME WITH YOUR CHILDREN
At the end of each week,
look and see where time was spent.

EARN YOUR CHILD'S EAR
Develop communication outside of just the negative.

DISCIPLINE WITH LOVE
Guidance and discipline are lacking today,
but be sure they are a function of
love and not just a reaction.

BE A ROLE MODEL
Because you are a role model!
Both sons and daughters will shape patterns and
expectations for the rest of their lives
based on their father's life.

BE A TEACHER

No one can replace what Dad alone can teach.

EAT TOGETHER AS A FAMILY

It is one of the easiest ways to bring everyone's days together, but so easy to crowd off the schedule.

READ TO YOUR CHILDREN

While many kids lean on technology, there should also be times when they learn from books and Dad together.

SHOW AFFECTION

Their security grows with each hug, kiss, evening wrestle, and prayer.

REALIZE THAT A FATHER'S JOB IS NEVER DONE

Time with them is short. Make the most of it.

MICHAEL HOWDEN
CONDENSED FROM "CHRISTIAN NEWS NORTHWEST"

# WAYS TO BE A BETTER MOM

❧

Pray *with* your children and *for* your children every day.

❧

Take time to listen to them individually. For younger children, sit on the floor, kneel down, or hold them on your lap so you can be at eye level.

❧

Give gentle hugs several times each day, and use endearing nicknames that make your children feel special.

❧

Compliment often, especially for good behavior and good character traits.

❧

Develop talents and giftedness by giving support and offering opportunities for your children to excel in these areas.

❧

Attend scholastic, sport, and church events. Volunteer to help in these areas.

Provide the tools and space for children to do homework. Follow up with teachers on a regular basis.

Encourage friendships that are a good influence; discourage those that are not.

Create a habit of letting your children know you love them when they wake up, go to sleep, leave, and come home.

Teach good manners, good grooming, respect for elders, and compassion and generosity for those that are less fortunate.

Attend church as a family.

Let your children see the affection and respect you and your husband have for each other.

ALICE GRAY
INSPIRATIONAL CONFERENCE SPEAKER

# PARENTING TIPS

- Set aside some time to make a list of the values you want to pass on to your children.
- Start a collection of good books about teaching values to children.
- Begin a prayer journal with each of your children.
- Teach your children that they must stand for something or they'll fall for anything.
- Have fun with your family, and watch for natural opportunities to talk about what's right and wrong.
- Bring back family dinner time.
- Get involved in a share group of parents with like-minded values.
- Talk casually and consistently with your children.

- Children are like sponges. They absorb our values and perceptions.

- Realize that kids won't buy a do-as-I-say-not-as-I-do philosophy. Honestly examine your own life.

- Walk out of movies that offend your values, and instruct your kids to do the same.

- Remember that if you allow TVs in your children's bedrooms, it's hard to monitor what they're watching.

- One of the greatest things you can do for your children is to make sure your marriage keeps getting better and better.

BILL AND KATHY PEEL
CONDENSED FROM "KINDRED SPIRIT" MAGAZINE

# HEALTHY FAMILIES...

*...are characterized by strong, supportive, honest communication.*

*...spend a large quantity of time together.*

*...share a common faith and practice.*

*...agree on key values.*

*...practice love and mutual appreciation.*

*...have common goals and interests.*

*...are able to negotiate solutions to crises.*

*...make sacrifices for the good of the family.*

*...exhibit trust among family members.*

ROBERT LEWIS
CONDENSED FROM "REAL FAMILY VALUES"

# 12 THINGS KIDS WORRY ABOUT

1. Will my parents stay together?
2. What if my parents die or get in an accident?
3. How can I keep my mom or dad from getting angry at me?
4. Will people at school like me?
5. Will I be able to do well at school?
6. What if my friends don't want to be my friends anymore?
7. Will my parents be able to pay all our bills?
8. Will I be safe today?
9. Do I look okay?
10. What if I get embarrassed?
11. What if someone hurts me or my family?
12. What does the future hold for me?

MIKE DEBOER
MIDDLE SCHOOL COUNSELOR

# HOW TO GET YOUR KIDS TO HELP AT HOME

**Start them young.**

The younger they learn to do chores, the less resistant they are to do them when they get older.

**Teach by example.**

Make sure your kids see you doing chores the way you expect them to be done—completely and with a positive attitude.

**Provide clear instructions.**

Give specific, understandable steps to complete each chore, and then patiently demonstrate how you want it done.

**Assign what's age appropriate.**

Be aware of what's reasonable to expect at each age. Because of coordination, strength, concentration, and general maturity, there are some jobs that kids must grow into.

**Make it visual.**

Write out job descriptions, assignment schedules, or check-off lists, and keep them posted where the kids will see them daily.

**Stick with a routine.**

Set up certain days and times to do chores. Then be consistent with maintaining your routines.

**Encourage teamwork.**

Work together in pairs or as an entire family on certain chores. With others involved, hard tasks seem much easier and get accomplished much faster.

**Reward chores done well.**

Acknowledge your kids' attitudes and effort. Show them your appreciation through verbal affirmation, prizes, allowance, or special family time.

**Trade chores.**

Whenever possible, rotate chores with different family members to allow for variety and to encourage all members to learn each job.

**Keep it fun.**

Turn chores into games or contests. Smiling, laughing, or singing makes work seem a lot less like work.

MONICA POWERS
CREATIVE ORGANIZER AND MOTHER OF THREE

# FIVE WAYS TO TEACH YOUR CHILD THE ART OF SHARING

1\.

Always look for ways to include your child in your gift giving and sharing.

2\.

Brainstorm with your child on ways to make a sad friend smile.

3\.

Make an action plan for sharing. Prepare an easy and age-appropriate plan so that the child may take an active role.

4\.

When delivering a gift, take the children with you and make them an important part of the delivery.

5\.

Be a model for your children by sharing your resources with a family that is less fortunate, donating clothes or supplies to natural-disaster victims, collecting toys for a toy drive, or baking a batch of cookies for a sick neighbor.

JANE JARRELL
FROM "MOM MATTERS"

# FIVE STEPS TO BETTER BEHAVIOR

*Be consistent.*

*Stay cool.*

*Clarify the consequences.*

*Be forgiving.*

*Overlook past offenses.*

GARY D. CHAPMAN
CONDENSED FROM "CHRISTIAN PARENTING TODAY"

# FOUR TIPS TO AVOID CLEANUP CONFLICT

1.

*Do I give my child advance warning before he must clean up?*

Children can become intensely involved in what they are doing. Your child will respond more positively if he is alerted in advance when play must end.

2.

*Do my child and I have the same definition of cleanup?*

Young children may define *cleanup* as tossing toys into the closet. You may define it as sorting toys into specific containers. Teach your child how to clean up by showing him how you want toys put away. Work alongside him for a couple of days to reinforce what he is to do.

3.

*Do I affirm my child when he puts away his toys?*

"Catch your child being good" is the basis of all child-management techniques. When you catch your child being good by putting away toys, he knows exactly what behavior you want him to repeat. Give specific praise the next time you see him box up his cars.

4.

*Do I occasionally make cleanup fun?*

Children love games. Designate one tape or CD as cleanup music. Then turn it on only when it's cleanup time. One day a child can clean half the room and you can clean the other half and see who gets done first. Or set up a race against the clock. For five days keep track of how quickly your child cleans up. He can race against himself.

MARY MANZ SIMON
CONDENSED FROM "THE YEAR-ROUND PARENT"

# SEVEN PRINCIPLES OF DISCIPLINE

1.
Establish a healthy authority over your children.

2.
Hold your children accountable for their actions.

3.
Let reality be the teacher.

4.
Use action more than words.

5.
Stick to your guns, but don't shoot yourself in the foot.

6.
Relationships come before rules.

7.
Live by your values.

DR. KEVIN LEMAN
ADAPTED FROM "MAKING CHILDREN MIND WITHOUT LOSING YOURS"

# GOOD MANNERS WHEN MEETING OTHERS

### STAND

Children should stand when they are introduced to someone their own age or to someone older.

### SMILE

Smiles are contagious. Give one and you get one in return. Smiles read the same on any face in any language.

### SEE THE COLOR OF THEIR EYES

If you feel self-conscious about looking people in the eye, look for the color of their eyes, or practice looking at yourself in the mirror until you feel comfortable doing so.

### SHAKE HANDS

Proper handshakes are firm, dry, and not too long.

### SAY HELLO

Say hello, and always say the person's name if you know it. To show respect, children should use a title and the last name, such as, "Hello, Mr. Kendall."

JUNE HINES MOORE
CONDENSED FROM "YOU CAN RAISE A WELL-MANNERED CHILD"

# 10 WAYS TO ENCOURAGE SELF-RELIANT BEHAVIOR

**1. Help Your Child Develop Confidence.**
When approaching new tasks, your child needs to feel a sense of confidence. The praise you offer consistently, specifically, and honestly will help your child begin new efforts with a sense of confidence.

**2. Present Your Child with Opportunities.**
He is continuing to develop new capabilities, better judgment, and increased skills that can be adapted and applied in a variety of settings.

**3. Admit That You Make Mistakes.**
If your child only sees you as "perfect," he may feel he can't ever be like that. Your child wants to be like you. You are the most important role model. Let your child see the authentic you.

**4. Have Realistic Expectations.**
A child will not make a bed perfectly the first time. He will need assistance and understanding before the bed looks neat. He may need additional time to gather his soccer gear before the first practice. Adjust your expectations to fit your child.

**5. Teach Your Child to Value Learning.**
Build rewards into a task. For example, a child who clips food coupons from the newspaper and organizes them might earn a percentage of the money saved.

**6. Ask Your Child If He'd Like to Learn Something.**
"What would you like to learn about cooking, washing windows, or cleaning tools in the garage?" You might be surprised! But this single question offers a wonderful opportunity to build on your child's own interests.

**7. Focus on Specific Tasks.**
Identify what your child can do now, and then look ahead to what he'll be ready to attempt at the next stage. This allows your child to build new skills onto what he already knows.

**8. Increase Each Child's Level of Responsibility.**
Consider your personal comfort levels as your child adds new areas of responsibility. Follow your personal parenting time line, but continually increase each child's responsibilities.

**9. Support Your Child As He Learns.**
If he is going to take out the garbage every morning before school, he might need to learn how to set an alarm clock that will wake him up five minutes earlier. If he has several tasks to complete on a weekend, show him how to make a list.

**10. Remind Your Child of New Areas of Competence.**
After a child has successfully learned something new, ask, "What did you learn from this?" Remind the child about his new areas of competence.

MARY MANZ SIMON
CONDENSED FROM "THE YEAR-ROUND PARENT"

# 10 TIPS TO TRIGGER TALKING

1. *Establish eye contact.* If you have a young child, that might mean kneeling down next to him. With a tween, you might sit together at the kitchen table.

2. *Listen more than talk.* It's tempting to open our mouths more often than our ears. However, we learn more if we listen.

3. *Avoid misunderstandings.* Instead of checking comprehension by asking, "Do you understand?" ask your child specific questions. For example, if you aren't sure your child heard you say, "Take the dog out for a walk before supper," follow up by asking, "What time are you taking the dog for a walk?"

4. *Ask productive questions.* When you want to learn something, avoid questions with a yes or no response. If you really want to know what happened during the day, ask, "With whom did you eat lunch today?" "What did you do in math?" or "What made you laugh today?"

5. *Say, "I love you."* We can show our child we love him in many different ways, but we must also speak the words. Tell your child at least once a day that you love him.

6. *Locate a private place.* Your child will talk with you more freely if he knows a sibling isn't peeking around the corner. When you want privacy, go into a room and close the door. Or, go to the car. Whether it's parked in the driveway or stopped in traffic, a car can be an excellent place for personal sharing.

7. *Don't compete.* Although your child can multitask, for higher quality communication eliminate distractions. Turn off the television, turn down the radio, and focus on the conversation.

8. *Avoid repetition.* When a child knows you'll say something only once, he'll learn to listen the first time. This single action will prevent an endless number of communication problems. Repeat only words of love.

9. *Be transparent.* You will emotionally connect with your child when your words reflect the feelings in your heart. When appropriate, share from your soul.

10. *Respect each child's style.* An individual reflects his personal pattern of communication. One child might chatter freely about everything; another might say only two words about the same experience. Respect these differences. Just make sure each child can share his feelings, thoughts, concerns, and dreams.

MARY MANZ SIMON
CONDENSED FROM "THE YEAR-ROUND PARENT"

# CHILD PROOFING AGAINST CHEAP THRILLS

- *Protect your children from stress.* Accept their limitations, academic and otherwise. Be understanding of their personalities, too. There's no greater motivation for children than knowing their parents love them for themselves.

- *Prevent your children from becoming self-centered.* When children occupy the family spotlight, they grow up feeling that their desires come first. When parents' needs are emphasized, youngsters learn social responsibility and become more sensitive to others' wants.

- *Establish your authority early on and discipline well.* Parental authority is the cornerstone of a child's sense of security. A child's unshakable belief that his parents are powerful people who can protect and provide for him under any and all circumstances liberates and energizes the child's potential for creativity and productivity.

- *Assign your children regular chores around the home.* Not only do chores help children learn basic domestic skills; they instill responsibility, feelings of accomplishment, and a sense of obligation and family loyalty, all of which help to prevent self-defeating behaviors like drug use.

- *Prevent the "I've got nothin' to do" syndrome.* Keep television watching to a minimum, and don't ever let it become your child's primary source of entertainment.

- *Keep toy purchases to a minimum.* Instead, help your children develop resourcefulness, the antidote to boredom and the key to any success story, by steering them toward creative activities and reading.

- *Give your kids a healthy say in how they use their discretionary time.* Today's parents have a tendency to overstructure their child's free time. But youngsters whose lives are constantly being organized by adults are likely to have difficulty learning how to use time wisely or creatively.

- *Help your children resist peer pressure and think for themselves.* Listen to them. There is no better insurance against the negative effects of peer pressure than open lines of communication between parent and child.

- *Maintain a good sense of humor about your child's mistakes and your own as well.* Nothing pushes teenagers away from their families quicker than parents who take "parenting" matters—and themselves—too seriously.

JOHN ROSEMOND
CONDENSED FROM "TEEN PROOFING"

# THINGS KIDS HATE TO HEAR

- Can't you do anything right?
- When will you ever learn?
- What is wrong with you?
- You are lazy.
- You are stupid.
- You are so immature.
- Who do you think you are?
- You'll be the death of me yet.
- Haven't I taught you anything?
- You're just no good.
- You'll never amount to anything.

- You got what you deserved.
- You need your head examined.
- Don't you care about anything?
- What makes you think you're so special?
- I've had it with you.
- All you ever do is cause trouble.
- Just wait until you have kids.
- Don't you ever listen?
- When are you going to start obeying me?
- If I've told you once, I've told you a million times…

MIKE DEBOER
MIDDLE SCHOOL COUNSELOR

# HELPING YOUR CHILDREN GET TO SLEEP

1.

***Be consistent.***

Set a regular bedtime, and try to hit it as often as possible.

2.

***Don't allow them to get overtired.***

The more tired they are, the harder it is for them to sleep.

3.

***Make their room comfortable.***

Provide a comfortable bed and a peaceful room with the right temperature and lighting.

4.

***Don't send them to their room as discipline.***

If they're sent to their room when they're in trouble, they might associate being sent to bed with punishment.

5.

***Develop calming activities.***

Do these during the hour before bedtime to settle them down.

6.

***Establish bedtime rituals.***

Consistent patterns—such as brushing teeth, bedtime stories, laying beside them, saying prayers—help prepare them for sleep.

7.

***Use music.***

Play music your children find calm, gentle, and relaxing. Play it nightly as they drift off to sleep.

8.

***Be calm but firm.***

Don't be manipulated about bedtime. But realize that if you become loud or upset, your kids will have a harder time getting to sleep.

DR. STEVE STEPHENS
PSYCHOLOGIST AND SEMINAR SPEAKER

# EIGHT WAYS TO HELP YOUR CHILD GET GOOD GRADES

1.

Provide a quiet spot for your child to do his homework—someplace other than his bedroom, where games, toys, or even a television compete for his attention.

2.

Minimize distractions by making homework a family activity.

3.

A better way to study is to have your child write down key concepts in her own words, then study those notes.

4.

Dress your child in his favorite, most comfortable outfit on the day of an exam. If he feels good about himself, chances are he'll do better on a test.

5.

Limit TV viewing and computer use the night before a big test—staring at a screen can tire kids out.

6.

Help your child get organized to prevent lost assignments.

7.

Develop a calendar of important events for the next thirty to ninety days. Students should have both short- and long-term goals. Include extracurricular activities on the calendar in addition to homework projects.

8.

Celebrate all successes. Your C+ student is now a B- student? Buy her a book or see a movie together. Little treats will motivate your daughter to continue to work hard in the future.

JOANNE VAN ZUIDAM
CONDENSED FROM "FAMILY CIRCLE" MAGAZIN

# SEVEN IRREDUCIBLE NEEDS

1. *Ongoing nurturing relationships*

   Every baby needs a warm, intimate relationship with a primary caregiver over a period of years, not months or weeks.

2. *Physical protection, safety, and regulation*

   Both in the womb and in infancy, children need an environment that provides protection from physical or psychological harm, chemical toxins, and exposure to violence.

3. *Experiences tailored to individual differences*

   Every child has a unique temperament. Tailoring early experiences to nurture a child's individual nature prevents learning and behavioral problems and enables a child to develop his or her full potential.

4. *Developmentally appropriate experiences*

   Children of different ages need care tailored to their stage of development. Unrealistic expectations can hinder a child's development.

5. *Limit-setting, structure, and expectations*

Children need structure and discipline. They need adults who empathize as well as set limits. They need expectations rather than labels and adults who believe in their potential but understand their weaknesses. They need incentive systems, not failure models.

6. *Stable, supportive communities and culture*

To feel whole and integrated, children need to grow up in a stable community. This means a continuity of values in family, peer groups, religion, and culture, as well as exposure to diversity.

7. *Protecting the future*

Meeting all these needs should be our highest priority. If we fail, we will jeopardize our children's future.

T. BERRY BRAZELTON AND STANLEY GREENSPAN
CONDENSED FROM "THE IRREDUCIBLE NEEDS OF CHILDREN"

# 10 WAYS TO RAISE CHILDREN THAT WILL USE DRUGS

1. Obey their demands. Give in to their tantrums. Deny them nothing. If they want it, indulge them.

2. Overlook, defend, or rescue them from the consequences of their negative behavior. Accept their excuses or blame others.

3. Disregard moral principles. Be dishonest. Involve your children in lying to or cheating others and taking pleasure in the misfortune of others.

4. Avoid touching, hugging, and taking time to interact with your children. Deny the existence of their emotional and social needs. Discourage them from expressing feelings, and isolate them from friends, organizations, and activities.

5. Ignore their worthwhile and constructive habits. Avoid complimenting or praising their efforts. Dwell on their weaknesses. Expect them to fail. Express hopelessness in their ability to succeed or to cope positively with life's stresses.

6. Pretend you never make mistakes or have problems. Expect perfection from your children. Judge them harshly if they make a mistake or misbehave.

7. Establish and enforce tough, rigid rules. Discourage thoughts and questions by demanding that they do what you want, when you want it done. Never help them think of ways to work through their own problems.

8. Keep children constantly on guard by being unpredictable. Become angry at an action one day and laugh at it the next. Avoid any kind of routine or tradition.

9. Remain uninformed about drugs and drug use. If you smoke, drink alcohol excessively, or use other drugs, make excuses, and deny your own use.

10. Above all else, discount your own value as a human being. Communicate anger and resentment toward life. Engage in self-indulgent, self-destructive behaviors.

LEAH DAVIES
CONDENSED FROM WWW.KELLYBEAR.COM

# FAMILY LOVE

*Showing kindness and affection*

11

# THE BOTTOM LINE

—When your children ask, "Who's in charge?" tell them.

—When they mutter, "Who loves me?" take them in your arms and surround them with affection.

—When they defiantly challenge you, win decisively. Talk to them. Set up clear boundaries and then enforce the rules firmly and fairly.

—Expose your children to interesting things. Help them use their time wisely.

—Raise them in a stable family with two parents who love each other and enjoy a strong marriage.

—Teach them to love the Lord and understand His Word.

—Treat them with respect and dignity and expect the same in return.

—Set aside time to build friendship and love between generations.

DR. JAMES AND SHIRLEY DOBSON
FROM "NIGHT LIGHT"

# WHAT DOES YOUR CHILD NEED MOST?

1. Hugs
2. Patience
3. Acceptance
4. To feel important
5. A sense of belonging
6. A sense of humor
7. Home—a safe haven
8. Common sense
9. Prayer
10. Laughter
11. Routine
12. Firm boundaries
13. To know Mom and Dad love each other
14. Freedom to fail
15. LOVE, LOVE, LOVE

ELISA MORGAN AND CAROL KUYKENDALL
FROM "WHAT EVERY CHILD NEEDS"

# WHAT HELPS YOU MEET YOUR CHILD'S NEEDS?

1. Counting to ten a lot
2. Listening
3. Watching
4. Using a softer tone of voice
5. Tearing up your to-do list
6. Being able to forgive—again and again
7. Turning off the TV
8. Taking a nap so you're rested
9. Using an answering machine more often
10. A microwave
11. Using paper plates sometimes
12. Noticing when your child does something right
13. Asking older parents lots of questions
14. Seizing the moment
15. NEVER GIVING UP

ELISA MORGAN AND CAROL KUYKENDALL
FROM "WHAT EVERY CHILD NEEDS"

# ENCOURAGING WORDS

1. Great! 2. You've got it. 3. You're on the right track now. 4. That's right. 5. Now you have the hang of it. 6. That a way! 7. You're doing just fine. 8. Now you have it! 9. You did it! 10. Fantastic! 11. Tremendous! 12. Terrific! 13. Wow! 14. Awesome! 15. How did you do that? 16. That's better. 17. Excellent! 18. That's the best you've ever done. 19. Keep it up. 20. That's so nice. 21. Keep up the good work. 22. Good job! 23. Much better. 24. Super! 25. Exactly. 26. You make it look so easy. 27. You can do it. 28. Way to go! 29. You're doing better. 30. Superb! 31. Wonderful! 32. You're the best! 33. No one does it better. 34. You're better every day. 35. I knew you could do it. 36. Keep working on it. 37. Beautiful! 38. The best! 39. Keep it up. 40. Nothing can stop you now. 41. You're great! 42. You made me proud. 43. You did that well. 44. That's it. 45. You're learning fast. 46. Perfect. 47. Fine. 48. Congratulations! 49. Outstanding! 50. Neat. 51. Remarkable! 52. Superstar! 53. Nice work! 54. Now you're flying! 55. Bravo! 56. Hurray for you! 57. You're on target. 58. How nice. 59. Hot dog! 60. Dynamite! 61. You're jazzed! 62. I like you. 63. Spectacular! 64. Great discovery. 65. Hip, hip, hurray! 66. Bingo! 67. Marvelous! 68. Phenomenal! 69. Exceptional performance! 70. A real trouper. 71. What a good listener. 72. You care. 73. I trust you. 74. You mean a lot to me. 75. You make me happy. 76. A-plus job! 77. You're a joy. 78. A-OK! 79. I like that smile. 80. Keep looking up. 81. Just perfect. 82. You're important. 83. Unbelievable! 84. How did you do that? 85. You're my friend. 86. You made my day! 87. The best! 88.You discovered the secret. 89. You're a darling. 90. Kudos! 91. I like the way you work. 92. Now that's a handshake! 93. You're beautiful! 94. I'm proud of you! 95. You're unique. 96. What a winner! 97. You know the secret. 98. I sure do love you.

KEN SUTTERFIELD
FROM "THE POWER OF AN ENCOURAGING WORD"

# 10 SIGNS OF A GREAT FAMILY

1. TOGETHERNESS
We enjoy spending time together.

2. RESPECT
We respect one another's thoughts,
feelings, boundaries, and possessions.

3. ACCEPTANCE, APPRECIATION, AND AFFIRMATION
We encourage and build one another up.

4. LOVE
We care about one another and communicate our love.

5. RULES AND RESPONSIBILITY
We follow certain rules and share family responsibilities.

6. COMMUNICATION
We talk to one another about what is on our hearts and minds.

7. FUN AND LAUGHTER
We relax and have good times together.

8. HONESTY
We are honest and truthful with one another.

9. TRADITIONS
We have routines, patterns, and traditions that bring us close.

10. FAITH
We have a common faith that gives us hope and
guides us through the easy and difficult times.

DR. STEVE STEPHENS
PSYCHOLOGIST AND SEMINAR SPEAKER

# EIGHT WAYS TO PRACTICE HUMOR

1. Keep a journal of ridiculous things that happen to your family.

2. Buy goofy joke books.

3. Encourage your kids to cut out and share their favorite newspaper comics.

4. Wite-Out the captions of cartoons, and have your kids write their own.

5. When you're under stress, look for the lighter side.

6. Develop a playful reaction to a problem.

7. Point out verbal humor like puns and oxymorons.

8. Keep a "lighten up" prop, like fake glasses and a nose, to don when things get tense.

FAITH TIBBETTS MCDONALD
CONDENSED FROM "CHRISTIAN PARENTING TODAY"

# HOW TO CHEER UP YOUR CHILDREN

§

*Hug them.*

§

*Listen to what they are saying.*

§

*Reassure them.*

§

*Set an example for them.*

§

*Allow them to cry.*

§

*Tell them it is okay to feel sad.*

CYNDI HAYNES
FROM "2002 WAYS TO CHEER YOURSELF UP"

# 17 WAYS TO ENCOURAGE READING

1.
Visit the library.

2.
Watch movies of classics.

3.
Create a reading nook.

4.
Listen to books on tape.

5.
Act out stories together.

6.
Be a reading role model.

7.
Get your child a journal to record her thoughts and read them again later.

8.
Read classic books aloud.

9.
Subscribe to children's magazines.

10.
Help your child write and illustrate his own book.

11.
Tolerate comic books.

12.
Keep reading time quiet.

13.
Pursue special interests through books.

14.
Attend a book signing.

15.
Break long books into manageable chunks.

16.
Visit bookstores.

17.
Introduce series books.

BARBARA CURTIS
FROM "READY, SET, READ!"

# BENEFITS WHEN YOUR CHILDREN ENJOY READING

*It can...*

widen horizons.

stimulate imagination.

counter the influence of television.

encourage the discovery of new interests.

strengthen family togetherness.

provide a storehouse of fond memories.

BOB HOSTETLER
CONDENSED FROM "RAISING CHILDREN BY THE BOOKS"
AS PUBLISHED IN "HOMELIFE" MAGAZINE

# GREAT FAMILY MEMORIES

### 1. Be a Secret Angel

Put everyone's name in a basket, and after dinner have each person draw a name. For the next week, each person must try to do a good deed or leave special surprises in secret for the other.

### 2. Classic Movie Night

For something fun on a cold winter's night, rent some movie classics, get out your fluffiest blankets and your slippers, and snuggle up.

### 3. For the Birds

Decorate one of your outdoor trees with food for the birds. Frost pinecones or jar lids with peanut butter, and tie them to the tree with colorful ribbons.

### 4. A Family Newspaper

Use candid photos of your daily life. Older children can review favorite books and report on recitals and games they've attended. A little one can draw a picture of the family pet. Photocopy and send to family and friends.

### 5. A "Homey" Hotel Vacation

Imagine that your home is a fine hotel. Give your "hotel" a name, and have the kids make up a sign to post on the front door. Stock your kitchen with food you love to order from room service. Then take turns being "the guest."

## 6. Tour Your Own Hometown

Think about places a tourist would visit in your community. Research points of interest and plan a day to play tourists!

## 7. Rainy-Day Fun

Don't let a rainy day spoil your fun! Start a rainy-day journal. Jot down things you'd like to do on a rainy day. Bring the list out whenever the sky turns gray.

## 8. Message of Love

Inflate a balloon, write a loving message on it with a permanent marker, and then deflate it. Tuck it into a lunch box, coat pocket, or purse to brighten your loved one's day.

## 9. The Nose Knows

Prepare a tray of foods in separate paper cups: a slice of lemon, a dab of mustard, garlic, taco sauce, green olives, etc. Blindfold your children and let them smell each food while guessing what it is.

## 10. The Time Capsule

Decorate a box with some of these items: a current newspaper and magazine, pictures and a video of you and your family; a favorite toy or baseball card; tape recordings; lists of your favorite movies, ice cream flavors, games, sports, etc. Then stash the box until it's time to rediscover the thoughts and memories of "way back then!"

RUTHANN WINANS AND LINDA LEE
CONDENSED FROM "101 IDEAS FOR MAKING FAMILY MEMORIES"

# 10 MORE WAYS TO BUILD A CLOSER FAMILY

1.
SNUGGLE TIME
Allow all the kids to come into bed with you one morning per week for a fifteen-minute snuggle time.

2.
BACKGROUND MUSIC
Set the atmosphere of your home by listening to uplifting, positive, or relaxing music.

3.
GAME PLAYING
Play board games (such as checkers, Monopoly, Parcheesi, Sorry).

4.
ONE AT A TIME
Once a week spend one hour with each child doing a favorite activity.

5.
SHORT TRIPS
When cabin fever has a grip, go somewhere for a little change of scenery, even if it's just for a drive.

6.
COUNTING BLESSINGS

At dinnertime or bedtime, sit down with your children and review three or four things for which you're thankful.

7.
HALF BIRTHDAYS

At the midpoint between birthdays, do something special to celebrate.

8.
SHARING HIGHS AND LOWS

Every evening ask your children about their high and low point of the day.

9.
MEDIA BLACKOUTS

One evening a week turn off all televisions, VCRs, radios, compact disc players, computers, and electronic equipment.

10.
SPECIAL DAYS

One day per month everybody in the family does kind and special things for a family member.

DR. STEVE STEPHENS
PSYCHOLOGIST AND SEMINAR SPEAKER

# EIGHT FOUNDATION BUILDERS FOR YOUR FAMILY

1\.
Hug and praise them.

2\.
See discipline as an asset.

3\.
Create traditions.

4\.
Cultivate laughter.

5\.
Stay close to teachers.

6\.
Be where they are.

7\.
Share your life with them.

8\.
Keep a long-range perspective.

SUSAN ALEXANDER YATES
FROM "HOW TO LIKE THE ONES YOU LOVE"

# SIX TYPES OF LOVE

1.
Hold-me-close love

2.
Crazy-about-me love

3.
Give-me-limits love

4.
Show-me-and-tell-me love

5.
Play-with-me love

6.
Help-me-hope love

ELISA MORGAN AND CAROL KUYKENDALL
FROM "WHAT EVERY CHILD NEEDS"

# 10 ESSENTIAL TOYS

1. PUZZLES

Fun for any age. They can provide hours of fun while teaching patience and logic.

2. A COSTUME TRUNK

Include clothespins and safety pins with discarded outfits to customize the fit. You can get all sorts of shoes and dress-up clothes at garage sales or thrift shops.

3. A CRAFT BOX

Include crayons, markers, scissors, stickers, glue sticks, string, and plenty of paper. Leave the kids alone and let their creativity bloom.

4. CARDBOARD BOXES

From shoe boxes to refrigerator boxes, it's amazing what kids can do. The more variety and number of boxes, the better. Add duct tape to join boxes and markers to decorate them.

5. LEGOS

Kids love these tiny plastic squares. They can build and create almost anything with these—cars, rocket ships, castles, houses, or entire cities. This isn't just for boys.

6. BALLS

You can kick them, throw them, shoot them, roll them, or even sit on them. Get as many sizes and styles as you can. Your kids will play with these from childhood through adulthood.

7. DOLLS

Give them clothes to change them, bottles to feed them, and blankets to keep them warm. Use a box with a pillow and a towel for a bassinet.

8. PUPPETS

Help your kids make their own hand puppets out of sock or papier-mâché. Use a table with a blanket over it as a stage. Then let the show begin!

9. BUG JAR AND MAGNIFYING GLASS

Go on a bug search, and examine what you find with the magnifying glass. Teach your kids to safely scoop up the critters and place them in a sealed, clear, plastic jar. Watch the bugs for a few hours, and then let them go.

10. PLAY MONEY AND A TOY CASH REGISTER

Play store and stock it with empty food boxes or cans. Provide a pen and stickers for pricing. Then take turns being the cashier or the customer.

MONICA POWERS
CREATIVE ORGANIZER AND MOTHER OF THREE

# THINGS TO DO WITH YOUR KIDS

## READ

Turn off the computer, the TV, and the CD or cassette player. Discover books.

## EXPLORE

Museums, historical sites, and even natural locations such as parks, beaches, mountains, and caves are great.

## INVENT

Cook, sew, build, invent.

## TRAVEL

Go somewhere you've never been before.

## LEARN

Learning new skills or improving a weak area can put your youngster ahead next year.

## PLAY

Life is pretty serious, even for kids, so there's nothing wrong in having some fun. But do it as a family.

## WORK

Learning to carry out responsibility is one of the most important lessons a kid can learn.

## WALK

Walking can be fun. It also gives you one-on-one time apart from the telephone, your schedule, and the noise of the TV.

## INVEST IN OTHERS

As a family, paint an elderly widow's house, or put a roof on the church. Reach out and do something for someone else.

## TOUCH GOD TOGETHER

Take time on a backpacking trip to focus on the beauty of what God has created, and as you build a fire and watch the stars, listen to your kids.

HAROLD SALA, PRESIDENT, GUIDELINES INTERNATIONAL MINISTRIES
CONDENSED FROM "GUIDELINES FOR LIVING" MAGAZINE

# RESPONSIBLE TV WATCHING

1\.

Be a positive example and use good judgment concerning the selection of television programs and movies to be viewed. Decide together which programs to watch.

2\.

Watch television with your child. Explain the difference between fact and fiction. If fighting occurs, comment that although the actors are pretending to be hurt, such violent acts in real life result in pain and suffering.

3\.

Turn the television and other objectionable media off when the material is contradictory to your family values. Explain to your child why you disapprove.

4.

Resist the temptation to put a television in your child's room. Instead, locate it where it can be monitored. If you family is on the Internet, keep the computer in a central location.

5.

Encourage your child to become involved in activities. Foster participation in hobbies, imaginative play, music, art, crafts, gardening, household tasks, yard work, cooking, and other worthwhile projects. Do more reading, walking, talking, listening, and playing together.

6.

Be an advocate for quality television programming. Join forces with other parents and teachers to set television-viewing guidelines.

LEAH DAVIES
CONDENSED FROM WWW.KELLYBEAR.COM

# PRAY FOR YOUR CHILDREN

*Pray for...*

their HEALTH.

their SAFETY.

their CHOICES.

their TEMPTATIONS.

their CONTENTMENT.

their FAITH.

their FRIENDS.

their CHARACTER.

their future MATE.

their LEGACY.

JOHN VAN DIEST
ASSOCIATE PUBLISHER

# NINE WORDS

*Never forget the nine most important words of any family—*

*I love you.*

*You are beautiful.*

*Please forgive me.*

H. JACKSON BROWN, JR.
FROM "LIFE'S LITTLE TREASURE BOOK ON MARRIAGE AND FAMILY"

# 12 GIFTS FOR YOUR CHILDREN

1. THE GIFT OF ATTENTION
I will watch and listen for your every need.

2. THE GIFT OF COMMUNICATION
I will take the time to know your heart and show you mine.

3. THE GIFT OF PATIENCE
I will slow down enough to walk beside you and let you be you.

4. THE GIFT OF HELP
I will assist you whenever things become too difficult for you to do alone.

5. THE GIFT OF ENCOURAGEMENT
I will believe the best in you, complimenting and praising you every chance I get.

6. THE GIFT OF PRAYER
I will pray for you day and night, in both good times and bad.

7. THE GIFT OF TEACHING

I will tell you in words you can hear and understand the life lessons you need to know.

8. THE GIFT OF FAITH

I will plant in you a picture of a loving God who sees all, hears all, knows all, and can do all.

9. THE GIFT OF DISCIPLINE

I will correct you firmly, consistently, and lovingly whenever the need arises.

10. THE GIFT OF EXAMPLE

I will be a model of virtue and character.

11. THE GIFT OF DIRECTION

I will show you a positive path to go and a positive way to walk it.

12. THE GIFT OF DREAMS

I will help you develop good dreams and teach you what it takes to successfully reach beyond the stars.

DR. STEVE STEPHENS
PSYCHOLOGIST AND SEMINAR SPEAKER

# IN THIS HOME

WE BELIEVE *in living deeply, laughing often, and loving always.*

WE BELIEVE *we were brought together to support and care for each other.*

WE BELIEVE *in celebrating together—our faith, our heritage, our traditions.*

WE BELIEVE *that everyone's feelings count and that the uniqueness of each of us strengthens all of us.*

WE BELIEVE *in the power of forgiveness to heal and the power of love to carry us through.*

WE BELIEVE *in one another, in this family, in this home.*

LISA O. ENGELHARDT
FROM "IN THIS HOME"

# WISDOM

## 12

*Learning from the experiences of others*

# CONTRASTS FOR LIFE

*Bitterness imprisons life;* LOVE RELEASES IT.

*Bitterness paralyzes life;* LOVE EMPOWERS IT.

*Bitterness sickens life;* LOVE HEALS IT.

*Bitterness blinds life;* LOVE ANOINTS ITS EYES.

HARRY EMERSON FOSDICK
FROM "RIVERSIDE SERMONS"

# BASIC RULES
## (FROM CHILDREN)

*Share.*
*Don't hit.*
*Stay on the path.*
*Don't chew with your mouth open.*
*Say "Please" and "Thank you."*
*Don't burp in public.*
*Be nice to old people.*
*Close your eyes when you pray.*
*Put your dishes in the sink.*
*Don't go through red lights.*
*Smile.*
*Hold hands when crossing the street.*
*Don't pick off scabs.*
*Brush your teeth.*
*Clean your room.*
*Listen.*
*Don't use bad words.*
*Don't call names.*
*Go to church.*
*Tell jokes.*
*Obey the rules.*

COLLECTED FROM CHILDREN AGES FIVE TO TEN

# WISDOM FOR ONE ANOTHER

- Love one another.
- Be kind to one another.
- Honor one another.
- Encourage one another.
- Confront one another.
- Comfort one another.
- Serve one another.
- Be patient with one another.
- Forgive one another.
- Pray for one another.

SAINT PETER, SAINT PAUL, AND SAINT JAMES
FROM "THE HOLY BIBLE"

# HOW TO LIVE

*Encourage one another.*

*Live in peace with each other.*

*Be patient with everyone.*

*Always try to be kind.*

*Be joyful evermore.*

*Pray continually.*

*In everything give thanks.*

*Hold on to good.*

*Avoid every kind of evil.*

SAINT PAUL THE APOSTLE
FROM "THE HOLY BIBLE"

# MEMORY

IT TEMPERS PROSPERITY,

CONSOLES ADVERSITY,

CAUTIONS YOUTH,

AND DELIGHTS OLD AGE.

AUTHOR UNKNOWN
QUOTED FROM "RIPPLES OF JOY"

# HEAR...SEE...DO...

I HEAR *and* I FORGET.

I SEE *and* I REMEMBER.

I DO *and* I UNDERSTAND.

CHINESE PROVERB

# 11 THINGS TO REMEMBER

The Value of Time

The Success of Perseverance

The Pleasure of Working

The Dignity of Simplicity

The Worth of Character

The Power of Kindness

The Influence of Example

The Obligation of Duty

The Wisdom of Economy

The Improvement of Talent

The Joy of Originating

RALPH HESS
SCHOOLTEACHER

# WORDS OF WISDOM

- Nothing great was ever achieved without enthusiasm.

- All I have seen teaches me to trust the Creator for all I have not seen.

- Trust men and they will be true to you; treat them greatly and they will show themselves great.

- If we encountered a man of rare intellect, we should ask him what books he read.

- Life is not so short but that there is always time enough for courtesy.

- Activity is contagious.

- Always do what you are afraid to do.

- The invariable mark of wisdom is to see the miraculous in the common.

- Our greatest glory consists not in never falling, but in rising up every time we fall.

- One of the most beautiful compensations of this life is that no one can sincerely try to help another without helping himself.

RALPH WALDO EMERSON
POET AND PHILOSOPHER

# PRAYER OF JABEZ

*I pray that…*

- You will bless me.
- You will enlarge my border.
- Your hand will be with me.
- You will keep me from harm.

FROM 1 CHRONICLES 4:10
"THE HOLY BIBLE"

# LET US LEARN BY PARADOX

- That the way down is the way up,
- That to be low is to be high,
- That the broken heart is the healed heart,
- That the contrite spirit is the rejoicing spirit,
- That the repenting soul is the victorious soul,
- That to have nothing is to possess all.

ARTHUR BENNETT
FROM "THE VALLEY OF VISION"

# PRAYER IS...

*...love's tender dialogue between the soul and God.*
JOHN RICHARD MORELAND

*...opening ourselves to God so that he can open us to others.*
LOUIS EVELY

*...the possibility to affect everything that affects us.*
E. M. BOUNDS

*...putting ourselves in the hands of God.*
MOTHER TERESA

*...the key of the morning and the bolt at night.*
AUTHOR UNKNOWN

*...the link that connects us with God.*
*It is the bridge that spans every gulf and carries*
*us safely over every chasm of danger or need.*
A. B. SIMPSON

*...the first step to meeting any challenge.*
RON MEHL

*...the central avenue God uses to transform us.*
RICHARD FOSTER

# EIGHT SIGNIFICANT CHOICES

1.
To resist pain or use it

2.
To gather wealth or gather grace

3.
To speak wisely or foolishly

4.
To value your time or fritter it away

5.
To live for self or for what is right

6.
To develop your talents or waste them

7.
To persevere or protest

8.
To stand for truth or abandon it

JILL BRISCOE
ADAPTED FROM "8 CHOICES THAT CAN CHANGE A WOMAN'S LIFE"

# DARE TO RISK

- To laugh is to risk appearing the fool.
- To weep is to risk appearing sentimental.
- To reach for another is to risk involvement.
- To expose your ideas, your dreams,
  before a crowd is to risk their loss.
- To love is to risk not being loved in return.
- To live is to risk dying.
- To believe is to risk failure.
- Only a person who risks is free.

AUTHOR UNKNOWN

# IT'S UP TO YOU

ONE SONG *can spark a moment,*

ONE FLOWER *can wake the dream.*

ONE TREE *can start a forest,*

ONE BIRD *can herald spring.*

ONE SMILE *begins a friendship,*

ONE HANDCLASP *lifts a soul.*

ONE STAR *can guide a ship at sea,*

ONE WORD *can frame the goal.*

ONE VOTE *can change a nation,*

ONE SUNBEAM *lights a room.*

ONE CANDLE *wipes out darkness,*

ONE LAUGH *will conquer gloom.*

ONE STEP *must start each journey,*

ONE WORD *must start each prayer.*

ONE HOPE *will raise our spirits,*

ONE TOUCH *can show you care.*

ONE VOICE *can speak with wisdom,*

ONE HEART *can know what's true,*

ONE LIFE *can make the difference.*

AUTHOR UNKNOWN

# TRY GOD

*When troubles are deep and your world is dark,*
*Don't give up hope*—TRY GOD.

*When life turns sour and you've lost your way,*
*Don't give up hope*—TRY GOD.

*When fears stack up and you're sure no one cares,*
*Don't give up hope*—TRY GOD.

*When temptation comes knocking and you struggle so,*
*Don't give up hope*—TRY GOD.

AUTHOR UNKNOWN

# TAKE TIME

**Take time to think;**
*it is the source of your power.*

**Take time to play;**
*it is the secret of your youth.*

**Take time to read;**
*it is the foundation of your knowledge.*

**Take time to dream;**
*it will take you to the stars.*

**Take time to laugh;**
*it really is your best medicine.*

**Take time to pray;**
*it is your touch with almighty God.*

**Take time to reach out to others;**
*it will give your life significance.*

GREGORY L. JANTZ, PH.D.
FROM "BECOMING STRONG AGAIN"

Life-changing advice in a quick-to-read format!

## *LISTS TO LIVE BY*

### LISTS TO LIVE BY

This treasury of to-the-point inspiration—two hundred lists—is loaded with invaluable insights for wives, husbands, kids, teens, friends, and more. These wide-ranging ideas can change your life!

ISBN 1-57673-478-1

### LISTS TO LIVE BY, THE SECOND COLLECTION

You'll get a lift in a hurry as you browse through this treasure-trove of more *Lists to Live By*—with wisdom for home, health, love, life, faith, and successful living.

ISBN 1-57673-685-7

# LOVE AND LOGIC FOR THE HAPPY COUPLE

LISTS TO LIVE BY FOR
EVERY MARRIED COUPLE

Offers tender, romantic, and wise ways to bring new life to marriage in a popular, easy-to-read format! This special collection of *Lists to Live By* is filled with gems of inspiration and timeless truths that married couples will treasure for a lifetime.

**ISBN 1-57673-998-8**

# SUCCESS STRATEGIES OF FAMILIES THAT FLOURISH

LISTS TO LIVE BY FOR
EVERY CARING FAMILY

Provides inspiration on how to love, teach, understand, uplift, and communicate with children in topics such as "Helping Your Child Succeed," "Pray for Your Children," and "Four Ways to Encourage Your Kids." Parents will cherish each nugget of truth in this timeless special collection of *Lists to Live By.*

**ISBN 1-57673-999-6**

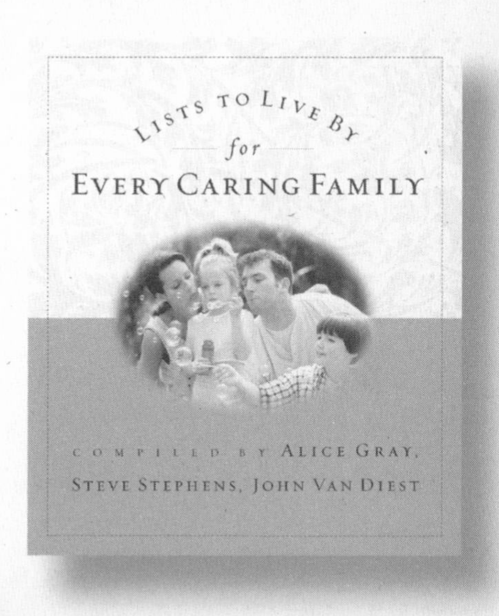

# The Stories for the Heart Series

compiled by Alice Gray

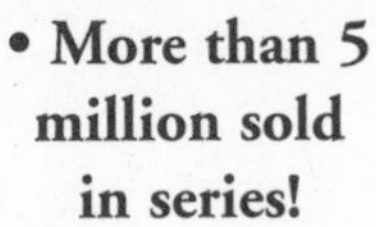


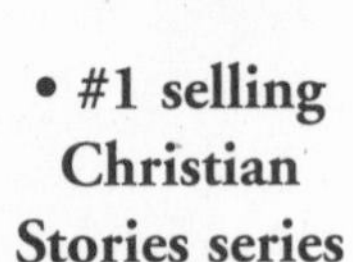

*Stories for the Extreme Teen's Heart* ........ *ISBN 1-57673-703-9*
*Stories for a Teen's Heart, Book 1* ........ *ISBN 1-57673-646-6*
*Stories for a Teen's Heart, Book 2* ........ *ISBN 1-57673-797-7*
*Stories for a Faithful Heart* ........ *ISBN 1-57673-491-9*
*Stories for a Woman's Heart, The First Collection* ........ *ISBN 1-57673-474-9*
*Stories for a Woman's Heart, The Second Collection* ........ *ISBN 1-57673-859-0*

*Stories for the Family's Heart* ........ *ISBN 1-57673-356-4*
*Stories for a Man's Heart* ........ *ISBN 1-57673-479-X*
*Stories for the Heart, The Original Collection* ........ *ISBN 1-57673-127-8*
*Stories for the Heart, The Second Collection* ........ *ISBN 1-57673-823-X*
*Stories for the Heart, The Third Collection* ........ *ISBN 1-57673-773-X*

www.storiesfortheheart.com

# ACKNOWLEDGMENTS

More than a thousand books and magazines were researched and dozens of professionals interviewed for this collection. A diligent effort has been made to attribute original ownership of each list and, when necessary, obtain permission to reprint. If we have overlooked giving proper credit to anyone, please accept our apologies. If you will contact Multnomah Publishers, Inc., Post Office Box 1720, Sisters, Oregon 97759, with written documentation, corrections will be made prior to additional printings.

Notes and acknowledgments are shown in the order the lists appear in each section of the book. For permission to reprint a list, please request permission from the original source shown in the following bibliography. The editors gratefully acknowledge the authors, publishers, and agents who granted permission for reprinting these lists.

## SUCCESS

"10 Actions for Staying Motivated" by Denis Waitley from *The Winner's Edge*. Copyright © 1986 Berkley Publishers/Random House, Inc. Used by permission.

"Nine Insights for Getting Ahead" from May 2000 issue of *Insights Newsletter.* Copyright © 2000. All rights reserved. Used by permission of The Meredith Agency on behalf of Insight for Living.

"How to Listen So People Will Talk" adapted from *Is There a Moose in Your Marriage?* by Nancy Cobb and Connie Grigsby. Published by Multnomah Publishers, Inc., Sisters, Oregon. Copyright © 2000. Used by permission.

"How to Talk So People Will Listen" by Dr. Steve Stephens, psychologist and seminar speaker. Copyright © 2001. Used by permission.

"A Personal Mission Statement..." condensed from *What Matters Most: The Power of Living Your Values* by Hyrum W. Smith. Copyright © 2000 by Franklin Covey Co. All rights reserved. Used with permission. www.franklincovey.com.

"People Who Have It Together Have..." condensed from *What Matters Most: The Power of Living Your Values* by Hyrum W. Smith. Copyright © 2000 by Franklin Covey Co. All rights reserved. Used with permission. www.franklincovey.com.

"Great Ways to Help Others Reach Their Goals" from *The Book of Change* by Cyndi Haynes. Copyright © 2000. Reprinted with permission of Andrews McMeel Publishing. All rights reserved.

"How to Keep Your Resolutions" by John Van Diest, associate publisher. Copyright © 2001. Used by permission.

"The Top 10 Mistakes Leaders Make" condensed from *The Top 10 Mistakes Leaders Make* by Hans Finzel. Copyright © 1994. Cook Communications Ministries, Colorado Springs, Colorado. Used by permission of the author.

"What a Leader Does" by Julie Baker from *Time Out for Women* magazine, copyright © 1999. Julie Baker is the founder of the national Christian women's organization Time Out for Women and author of *Time out for Prayer* (2000) and *A Pebble in the Pond* (2001), Chariot Victor Publishing, Colorado Springs, Colorado. Used by permission of the author.

"Am I Teachable?" by Marty Williams © 2001. Used by permission of the author.

"Those Who Attain Their Goals Are..." from *The Book of Change* by Cyndi Haynes. Copyright © 2000. Reprinted with permission of Andrews McMeel Publishing. All rights reserved.

"Put Space in Your Schedule" by Charles Lowery from *HomeLife* magazine, December 2000. Used by permission of the author. For more resources, contact www.CharlesLowery.com.

"Conquer Your Mountain of Clutter" by Dianna Booher from *Get a Life without Sacrificing Your Career.* Used by permission of the author. Dianna Booher, CEO of Booher Consultants, a communication training firm (written, oral, interpersonal, customer service), is author of *Get a Life, Communicate with Confidence!, The Worth of a Woman's Words,* and *Well Connected.* 800-342-6621. www.booherconsultants.com.

"Golden Threads of a Successful Life" from *Life Is Tremendous* by Charlie E. Jones. Copyright © 1968. Used by permission of the author, president of Life Management Services, Inc.

"Success Principles" condensed from *The Entrepreneur's Creed* by Merrill Oster and Mike Hamel. Copyright © 2001. Broadman & Holman Publishers, Inc., Nashville, Tennessee. Used by permission of the publisher.

"Nine Communication Skills" from *Speaking with Bold Assurance: How to Become a Persuasive Communicator* by Bert Decker and Hershael W. York. Copyright © 2001. Broadman & Holman Publishers, Inc., Nashville, Tennesee. Used by permission of the authors.

"The Way to Success" by Loren Fischer. Copyright © 2001. Used by permission of the author.

## FRIENDSHIP

"10 Things Friends Communicate" adapted from *Never Alone* by David and Teresa Ferguson. Copyright © 2001 by Intimate Life Ministries. Used by permission of Tyndale House Publishers. All rights reserved.

"Five Great Ways to Find a Friend" by Rhonda Rhea condensed from *Today's Christian Woman* magazine, March/April 2001. Used by permission of the author. Rhonda Rhea is a columnist for Christian publications in the U.S. and Canada and has also written many feature articles. She lives in the St. Louis area with her pastor husband and five children. RRhea@juno.com.

"Are You Too Sensitive?" from *How to Get Your Husband to Talk to You* by Nancy Cobb and Connie Grigsby. Published by Multnomah Publishers, Inc., Sisters, Oregon. Copyright © 2001. Used by permission.

"How to Be Friendly to Your Neighbors" from *Touched by Kindness.* Copyright © 2001 by Kim Boyce and Heidi Hess Saxton. Published by Servant Publications, P.O. Box 8617, Ann Arbor, Michigan 48107. Used with permission.

"When in Crisis, Find Good Friends Who..." reprinted from *Living through Personal Crisis* by Ann Kaiser Stearns. Copyright © 1984, by permission of Thomas More Publishing, 200 East Bethany Drive, Allen, Texas 75000.

"Five Principles for Authentic Communication" from *Boy Meets Girl* by Joshua Harris. Published by Multnomah Publishers, Inc., Sisters, Oregon. Copyright © 2000. Used by permission.

"Mutual Exchange" taken from *Groups: The Life-Giving Power of Community* by John Ortberg, Judson Poling, and Laurie Pederson. Copyright © 2000 by the Willow Creek Association. Used by permission of Zondervan Publishing House.

"Loving Ideas" condensed from *The Call to Love* by Linda Riley. Copyright © 2000. Used by permission of Tyndale House Publishers. All rights reserved.

"Sincere Friends" by Sheri Rose Shepherd from *Fit for Excellence,* copyright © 1998, by Creation House, Lake Mary, Florida. Used by permission.

"Superficial Friends" by Sheri Rose Shepherd from *Fit for Excellence,* copyright © 1998, by Creation House, Lake Mary, Florida. Used by permission.

"The Nature of Friendship" condensed from *The Marriage You've Always Wanted* by Tim and Julie Clinton. Copyright © 2000, Word Publishing, Nashville, Tennessee. All rights reserved. Used by permission.

"How to Help a Friend Who Is Depressed" condensed from *The Harder I Laugh, the Deeper I Hurt* by Stan Toler and Debra White Smith. Copyright © 2001, Beacon Hill Press of Kansas City. Used by permission.

"Your Best Friend" from *I Love You...Still* by Martha Bolton. Copyright © 2000. Published by Fleming H. Revell, a division of Baker Book House Company. Used by permission.

## VIRTUE

"Do Less" reprinted from *Smile for No Good Reason* by Lee L. Jampolsky, copyright © 2000 by Lee L. Jampolsky. Used by permission of Hampton Roads Publishing Company, Inc., Charlottesville, Virginia.

"Solitude Is a Place Where..." by Dr. Steve Stephens, psychologist and seminar speaker. Copyright © 2001. Used by permission.

"Better Your Life" by Paul Borthwick from *Discipleship Journal,* July/August 2000. Used by permission of the author, who is a senior consultant with Development Associates International.

"A Maturity Test" condensed from *After Every Wedding Comes a Marriage* by Florence and Fred Littauer. Copyright © 1981. Harvest House Publishers, Eugene, Oregon. Used by permission of the authors.

"Greed and Generosity" reprinted by permission of Thomas Nelson Publishers from the book entitled *Fatal Distractions,* copyright © 2000, by Ed Young.

"The Virtue of Discipline" taken from *If Mama Ain't Happy, Ain't Nobody Happy.* Copyright © 1996 by Lindsey O'Connor. Published by Harvest House Publishers, Eugene, Oregon 97402. Used by permission.

"A Question of Character" condensed from *A Question of Character* by Thad A. Gaebelein and Ron P. Simmons. Published by Hatherleigh Press, Long Island City, New York. Used by permission.

"Code of Character" from Major Scott Buchmann, as listed in *Christian Parenting Today* magazine, May/June 2001. Used by permission. Major Scott Buchmann is a professor of Military Science of the U.S. Army and director of Wheaton College's ROTC program.

"Peaceable Living" by Glenda Hotton, MA, CDC, MFT, counselor specializing in women's issues of trauma, abuse, relationships, and substance abuse. She is in private practice in Santa Clarita, California. Used by permission.

## HEALTH

"Seven Steps to Greater Health" taken from *Greater Health God's Way* by Stormie O'Martian. Copyright © 1999 by Harvest House Publishers, Eugene, Oregon 97402. Used by permission.

"10 Commandments of Great Nutrition" from *We Live Too Short and Die Too Long* by Walter Bortz II, MD. Copyright © 1991. Used by permission of Random House, Inc., New York, New York.

"Safety Tips from Your Pharmacist" by the Food and Drug Administration.

"14 Ways to Get Up on the Right Side of the Bed" by Becky Stephens, RN, Clackamas, Oregon. Copyright © 2001. Used by permission of the author.

"Getting Better Sleep" by Amy Givler from *HomeLife* magazine, December 2000. Copyright © 2000 LifeWay Christian Resources of the Southern Baptist Convention. All rights reserved. Used by permission.

"Five Ways to Reduce Stress" condensed from *The Year-Round Parent,* copyright © 2001 by Mary Manz Simon. Published by Servant Publications, P.O. Box 8617, Ann Arbor, Michigan 48107. Used with permission.

"Eight Steps for Healthy Walking" by George L. Baker condensed from *LifeWise* magazine, August/September 2000. Used by permission of the author. George L. Baker is a retired minister living in Sun City, Arizona.

"Workout Rewards" condensed from *Fabulous after 50* by Shirley Mitchell. Copyright © 2000. Published by New Leaf Press. Used by permission.

"Anger-Management Skills" condensed from *She's Gonna Blow!* Copyright © 2001 by Julie Ann Barnhill. Published by Harvest House Publishers, Eugene, Oregon 97402. Used by permission.

"Help for Headaches" by Amy Givler condensed from *HomeLife* magazine, March 2001. Copyright © 2001 LifeWay Christian Resources of the Southern Baptist Convention. All rights reserved. Used by permission.

"The Symptoms of Menopause" condensed from *Menopause and Mid-Life* by Robert Wells, MD, and Mary Wells. Copyright © 1994. Used by permission of Tyndale House Publishers. All rights reserved.

"Tips for Dealing with Hot Flashes" excerpted from *About...Menopause*, a *Life Advice®* pamphlet produced by MetLife's Consumer Education Center. Copyright © 1998 Metropolitan Life Insurance Company, New York, New York. Used by permission. All rights reserved. To order a free copy of this booklet or any of the over eighty *Life Advice®* pamphlets, call 1-800-METLIFE, or visit our Web site at www.metlife.com.

"Eating Right" by Amy Givler from *HomeLife* magazine, March 2001. Copyright © 2001 LifeWay Christian Resources of the Southern Baptist Convention. All rights reserved. Used by permission.

"Seven Ways to Take a Daily Minivacation" condensed from *Mom Matters*. Copyright © 2001 by Jane Jarrell. Published by Harvest House Publishers, Eugene, Oregon 97402. Used by permission.

"Having a Healthy Retirement" by The National Institute of Health.

"10 Commandments for Fitness" from *Staying Fit after Forty* by Andrew Seddon, MD. © 2001. Used by permission of SHAW/WaterBrook Press, Colorado Springs, Colorado. All rights reserved.

"12 Symptoms You Should Never Ignore" by Kevin McCurry, MD. Copyright © 2001. Used by permission of the author.

## MARRIAGE AND ROMANCE

"What Marriage Isn't" condensed from *Still the One* by Martha Bolton. Copyright © 2001. Published by Fleming H. Revell, a division of Baker Book House Company. Used by permission.

"Are You a Great Marriage Partner?" by Alice Gray, Dr. Steve Stephens, and John Van Diest. Copyright © 2001. Used by permission.

"12 Rules for a Happy Marriage" by Ann Landers. Permission granted by Ann Landers and Creators Syndicate.

"Little Things for Wives to Do" taken from *Marriage, Family, and Sexuality* by Kerby Anderson. Copyright © 2000, Kregel Publications, Grand Rapids, Michigan. Used by permission. All rights reserved.

"Little Things for Husbands to Do" taken from *Marriage, Family, and Sexuality* by Kerby Anderson. Copyright © 2000, Kregel Publications, Grand Rapids, Michigan. Used by permission. All rights reserved.

"Seven Commitments for a Strong Marriage" by Dr. Steve Stephens, psychologist and seminar speaker. Copyright © 2001. Used by permission.

"Remember to Listen" quoted from *Two Hearts Are Better than One* by Dennis and Barbara Rainey. Copyright © 1999 by Dennis and Barbara Rainey. Used by permission of J. Countryman, a division of Thomas Nelson, Inc.

"How Well Do We Communicate?" adapted from *After Every Wedding Comes a Marriage* by Florence and Fred Littauer. Copyright © 1997 by Harvest House Publishers, Eugene, Oregon 97402. Used by permission.

"What If..." condensed from *Still the One* by Martha Bolton. Copyright © 2001. Published by Fleming H. Revell, a division of Baker Book House Company. Used by permission.

"10 Reasons Why Divorce Isn't the Answer" by Dr. Steve Stephens, psychologist and seminar speaker. Copyright © 2001. Used by permission.

"Seven Steps to Prevent Divorce" condensed from *Family Shock* by Gary C. Collins. Copyright © 1995. Used by permission of the author.

"Marital Dating" by Alice Gray, Dr. Steve Stephens, and John Van Diest. Copyright © 2001. Used by permission.

"Questions for Sharing Your Dreams and Hopes" selected from *Two Hearts Are Better than One* by Dennis and Barbara Rainey. Copyright © 1999 by Dennis and Barbara Rainey. Used by permission of J. Countryman, a division of Thomas Nelson, Inc.

"Gifts for Your Spouse" by Dr. Steve Stephens, psychologist and seminar speaker. Copyright © 2001. Used by permission.

## CONTENTMENT

"15 Ways to Cheer Yourself Up" condensed from *2002 Ways to Cheer Yourself Up* by Cyndi Haynes. Copyright © 1998. Reprinted with permission of Andrews McMeel Publishing. All rights reserved.

"Keeping Joy in Your Life" condensed from *A Cup of Hope* by Emilie Barnes. Copyright © 2000 by Emilie Barnes. Published by Harvest House Publishers, Eugene, Oregon 97402. Used by permission.

"18 Ways to Feel Better" condensed from *Sometimes I Wake Up Grumpy…and Sometimes I Let Him Sleep* by Karen Scalf Linamen. Copyright © 2001. Published by Fleming H. Revell, a division of Baker Book House Company. Used by permission of the publisher.

"How to Be Happier Every Day" by Joan Lunden from *Wake-Up Calls* as quoted in *Family Circle* magazine, November 1, 2000. Reproduced with permission of The McGraw-Hill Companies.

"Less Is More" by Karen Hayse. Copyright © 2001. Condensed from www.maxedout.net. Used by permission of the author.

"Slow Down And…" reprinted from *Smile for No Good Reason* by Lee L. Jampolsky, copyright © 2000 by Lee L. Jampolsky. Used by permission of Hampton Roads Publishing Company, Inc., Charlottesville, Virginia.

"Positive Principles" condensed from *Living beyond Your Lifetime* by Mike Huckabee. Copyright © 2000. Published by Broadman & Holman Publishers, Inc., Nashville, Tennessee. Used by permission.

"Appreciating Good Days" from *A Cup of Hope* by Emilie Barnes. Copyright © 2000 by Emilie Barnes. Published by Harvest House Publishers, Eugene, Oregon 97402. Used by permission.

"How to Be Really Content" by Karen L. Willoughby. Copyright © 2001. Used by permission of the author, who is a writer, editor, and writing coach in Vancouver, Washington.

"Eight Proven Steps toward Feeling Good" from *2002 Ways to Cheer Yourself Up* by Cyndi Haynes. Copyright © 1998. Reprinted with permission of Andrews McMeel Publishing. All rights reserved.

## LIFE

"If I Could Live Life All Over Again…" from *The Marriage You've Always Wanted* by Tim and Julie Clinton. Copyright © 2000, Word Publishing, Nashville, Tennessee. All rights reserved. Used by permission.

"Taming Fears" condensed from *Sometimes I Wake Up Grumpy…and Sometimes I Let Him Sleep* by Karen Scalf Linamen. Copyright © 2001. Published by Fleming H. Revell, a division of Baker Book House Company. Used by permission of the publisher.

"Mending a Broken Heart" by Marty Williams. Copyright © 2001. Used by permission of the author.

"Four Qualities of Hardy People" adapted from *A Burden Shared* by Jane Kirkpatrick. Copyright © 1998. Used by permission of the author.

"Surviving Bad Days" from *A Cup of Hope* by Emilie Barnes. Copyright © 2000 by Emilie Barnes. Published by Harvest House Publishers, Eugene, Oregon 97402. Used by permission.

"Things I Wish I Knew When I Was Younger" by Laura Manske condensed from *McCall's* magazine, November 1998. Used by permission of the author. Laura Manske is deputy editor of *Family Life* magazine and author of *Family Travel: The Farther You Go, the Closer You Get,* published by Travelers' Tales, Inc.

"Secrets to Living Beyond 90" compiled by Steve Stephens, psychologist and seminar speaker. Copyright © 2001. Used by permission.

"Why Older is Better" compiled by Alice Gray, Steve Stephens, and John Van Diest. Copyright © 2001. Used by permission.

"10 Commandments for a Successful Retirement" by L. James and Jackie Harvey condensed from *Every Day Is Saturday: A Christian Guide to a Fantastic Retirement*. Concordia Publishing House, copyright © 2000. Used by permission of the author.

"Activities for a Great Retirement" excerpted from *About...Enjoying Retirement*, a *Life Advice®* pamphlet produced by MetLife's Consumer Education Center. Copyright © 1998, Metropolitan Life Insurance Company, New York, New York. Used by permission. All rights reserved. To order a free copy of this booklet or any of the over eighty *Life Advice®* pamphlets, call 1-800-METLIFE, or visit our Web site at www.metlife.com.

"Myths about Aging" from *The Nine Myths of Aging: Maximizing the Quality of Later Life,* copyright © 1998 by Douglas H. Powell. W. H. Freeman and Company, New York. Used by permission.

"Myths about Grief" by Dr. Steve Stephens, psychologist and seminar speaker. Copyright © 2001. Used by permission.

"Gifts to Give Yourself during Bereavement" from *A Passage through Grief* by Barbara Baumgardner. Copyright © 1997. Used by permission of the author.

"How to Help Me as I Grieve" by Providence Home and Community Services—Community Care Project, Portland, Oregon. Used by permission.

"Five Lessons for Life" by Marian Wright Edelman condensed from *Parade* magazine, October 24, 1999. Copyright © Marian Wright Edelman. Reprinted with permission of *Parade* magazine, copyright © 1999, and the author.

"50 Great Goals for the New Year" by Alice Gray, Dr. Steve Stephens, and John Van Diest. Copyright © 2001. Used by permission.

## HOME AND FINANCE

"Proper Money Management" from *The Financially Confident Woman* by Mary Hunt. Copyright © 1996. Published by Broadman & Holman Publishers, Inc., Nashville, Tennessee. Used by permission of the publisher.

"How to Recognize a Risky Investment" from *Getting out of Debt* by Howard L. Dayton Jr. Copyright © 1986. Used by permission of Tyndale House Publishers. All rights reserved.

"Warning Signs That You Need Financial Counseling" by Mary McLean Hix condensed from *HomeLife* magazine, December 2000. Used by permission of the author. Mary McLean Hix is a freelance writer from Lakeland, Florida.

"Teaching Kids to Handle Money" by Ken Canfield condensed from *Today's Father* magazine 8, no. 2. Used by permission of the publisher. Ken Canfield is founder and president of the National Center for Fathering. For tips and resources on fathering, visit the center's Web site at www.fathers.com.

"Practical Lessons with Money" by Ken Canfield condensed from *Today's Father* magazine 8, no. 2. Used by permission of the publisher. Ken Canfield is founder and president of the National Center for Fathering. For tips and resources on fathering, visit the center's Web site at www.fathers.com.

"15 Ways to Spend Less Money" condensed from *The Financially Confident Woman* by Mary Hunt. Copyright © 1996. Published by Broadman & Holman Publishers, Inc., Nashville, Tennessee. Used by permission of the publisher.

"Financial Perspective" by John Van Diest, associate publisher. Copyright © 2001. Used by permission.

"10 Ways to Save on Gasoline" by Bob Cerullo from *Parade* magazine, July 9, 2000. Reprinted with permission of the author and of *Parade* magazine, copyright © 2000.

"Travel Tips" by Yvonne Beeman from *Senior Life* magazine, January 2001. Used by permission of the publisher.

"Letting Go of the Family Home" by Judith D. Schwartz condensed from *New Choices* magazine, October 2000. Used by permission of the author. www.newchoices.com.

"How to Do (Almost) Everything" by Jeanne Zornes adapted from *Today's Christian Woman* magazine, January/February 2001. Used by permission of the author. Jeanne Zornes, of Wenatchee, Washington, is author of hundreds of articles and seven books including *Spiritual Spandex for the Outstretched Soul* (Shaw/WaterBrook, 2000).

"De-Junking Your Home" reprinted from *How to Handle 1,000 Things at Once*. Copyright © 1997 by Don Aslett. Reprinted with permission of Betterway Books, an imprint of F&W Publications, Inc. All rights reserved.

"Five Ways to Keep Your Home Running Smoothly" from *Mom Matters*. Copyright © 2001 by Jane Jarrell. Published by Harvest House Publishers, Eugene, Oregon 97402. Used by permission.

"12 Time-Management Tips for Your Home" excerpted from Pat Abernathy's time-management seminar, "Time-Management Solutions for Overly Busy Women!" Copyright © 2000. Used by permission of the author.

"What Every Family Member Needs to Know" by Pat Van Diest, RN. Copyright © 2001. Used by permission.

## TEENS

"Every Teen Struggles With..." by Holmbeck, Paikoff, and Brooks-Gunn from *Handbook of Parenting: Applied and Practical Parenting* as published in *Five Cries of Parents* by Merton and Irene Strommen. Used by permission of the authors.

"Five Items Kids Say They Want" from *The Disconnected Generation* by Josh McDowell. Copyright © 2000, Word Publishing, Nashville, Tennessee. All rights reserved. Used by permission.

"Six Critical Parent-Teen Issues" condensed from *Teen Proofing* by John Rosemond, author and family psychologist. Copyright © 2001, Andrews McMeel Publishing. Used by permission of the author.

"Common Misconceptions about Building Self-Esteem" by Christy Heitger-Casbon condensed from *HomeLife* magazine, January 2001. Used by permission of the publisher.

"How to Build Your Teenager's Self-Esteem" by Christy Heitger-Casbon condensed from *HomeLife* magazine, January 2001. Used by permission of the publisher.

"Connecting with Teens" from *The Disconnected Generation* by Josh McDowell. Copyright © 2000, Word Publishing, Nashville, Tennessee. All rights reserved. Used by permission.

"Adults Who Are Most Successful with Teens..." reprinted from *Teenage Boys!* Copyright © 1998 by William J. Beausay II. Used by permission of WaterBrook Press, Colorado Springs, Colorado. All rights reserved.

"Six Principles of Intentional Parenting" reprinted from *Teenage Boys!* Copyright © 1998 by William J. Beausay II. Used by permission of WaterBrook Press, Colorado Springs, Colorado. All rights reserved.

"Prepare Your Teen for the Unexpected" used with permission from *Coaching Your Kids in the Game of Life* by Ricky Byrdsong. Copyright © 2000, Bethany House Publishers.

"Rules for Parent-Teen Communication" taken from *Helping the Struggling Adolescent* by Dr. Les Parrott III. Copyright © 1993 by Les Parrott III. Used by permission of Zondervan Publishing House.

"Do's and Don'ts for Better Conversations with Teens" reprinted with the permission of Simon & Schuster from *Speaking Your Mind in 101 Difficult Situations* by Don Gabor. Copyright © 1994 by The Stonesong Press, Inc.

"What Teens Look for in a Job" from *Life Skills for Guys* by Tim Smith. Copyright © 2000 Cook Communications Ministries. Copied with permission. May not be further reproduced. All rights reserved.

"How to Spot Depression in Teens" by Wesley Sharpe, Ed.D., from *HomeLife* magazine, December 2000. Used by permission of the author.

"Dealing with a Dating Teen" by Ann B. Gannon condensed from *HomeLife* magazine, February 2001. Used by permission.

"A Teenager's 10 Agreements" reprinted from *Teenage Boys!* Copyright © 1998 by William J. Beausay II. Used by permission of WaterBrook Press, Colorado Springs, Colorado. All rights reserved.

"Does Your Teen Need Professional Help?" taken from *Helping the Struggling Adolescent* by Dr. Les Parrott III. Copyright © 1993 by Les Parrott III. Used by permission of Zondervan Publishing House.

"When It's Time to Let Go" by Howard and Jeanne Hendricks condensed from *Kindred Spirit* magazine. Used by permission of the authors. Howard Hendricks is the distinguished professor and chairman for the Center for Christian Leadership at Dallas Theological Seminary.

## FAMILY LESSONS

"Every Child Needs..." by Leah Davies condensed from Kelly Bear Web site. www.kellybear.com.

"Ways to Be a Better Dad" by Michael Howden condensed from *Christian News Northwest*. Used by permission of the author. Michael Howden is the executive director of the Oregon Center for Family Policy.

"Ways to Be a Better Mom" by Alice Gray, inspirational conference speaker. Copyright © 2001. Used by permission.

"Parenting Tips" by Bill and Kathy Peel condensed from *Kindred Spirit* magazine. Copyright © 1995. Used by permission of the authors.

"Healthy Families..." condensed from *Real Family Values* by Robert Lewis. Published by Multnomah Publishers, Inc., Sisters, Oregon. Copyright © 1995, 2000. Used by permission.

"12 Things Kids Worry About" by Mike DeBoer, middle school counselor. Copyright © 2001. Used by permission of the author.

"How to Get Your Kids to Help at Home" by Monica Powers, a creative organizer and mother of three. Copyright © 2001. Used by permission of the author.

"Five Ways to Teach Your Child the Art of Sharing" from *Mom Matters*. Copyright © 2001 by Jane Jarrell. Published by Harvest House Publishers, Eugene, Oregon 97402. Used by permission.

"Five Steps to Better Behavior" by Gary D. Chapman condensed from *Christian Parenting Today* magazine, July/August 1999. Used by permission of the author. Gary D. Chapman, Ph.D., is the author of *Five Signs of a Loving Family* (Northfield Publishing).

"Four Tips to Avoid Cleanup Conflict" condensed from *The Year-Round Parent*, copyright © 2001 by Mary Manz Simon. Published by Servant Publications, P.O. Box 8617, Ann Arbor, Michigan 48107. Used with permission.

"Seven Principles of Discipline" adapted from *Making Children Mind without Losing Yours* by Dr. Kevin Leman. Copyright © 1984. Published by Fleming H. Revell, a division of Baker Book House Company. Used with permission.

"Good Manners When Meeting Others" condensed from *You Can Raise a Well-Mannered Child* by June Hines Moore. Copyright © 1996. Published by Broadman & Holman Publishers, Inc., Nashville, Tennessee. Used with permission.

"10 Ways to Encourage Self-Reliant Behavior" condensed from *The Year-Round Parent*, copyright © 2001 by Mary Manz Simon. Published by Servant Publications, P.O. Box 8617, Ann Arbor, Michigan 48107. Used with permission.

"10 Tips to Trigger Talking" condensed from *The Year-Round Parent*, copyright © 2001 by Mary Manz Simon. Published by Servant Publications, P.O. Box 8617, Ann Arbor, Michigan 48107. Used with permission.

"Child Proofing against Cheap Thrills" condensed from *Teen Proofing* by John Rosemond, author and family psychologist. Copyright © 2001, Andrews McMeel Publishing. Used by permission of the author.

"Things Kids Hate to Hear" by Mike DeBoer, middle school counselor. Copyright © 2001. Used by permission of the author.

"Helping Your Children Get to Sleep" by Dr. Steve Stephens, psychologist and seminar speaker. Copyright © 2001. Used by permission.

"Eight Ways to Help Your Child Get Good Grades" by Joanne Van Zuidam condensed from *Family Circle* magazine, September 12, 2000. Reprinted with the permission of *Family Circle* magazine.

"Seven Irreducible Needs" condensed from *The Irreducible Needs of Children* by T. Berry Brazelton and Stanley Greenspan. Copyright © 2000 by. T. Berry Brazelton and Stanley Greenspan. Reprinted by permission of Perseus Books Publishers, a member of Perseus Books, LLC.

"10 Ways to Raise Children That Will Use Drugs" by Leah Davies condensed from Kelly Bear Web site. www.kellybear.com.

## FAMILY LOVE

"The Bottom Line" from *Night Light* by Dr. James and Shirley Dobson. Published by Multnomah Publishers, Inc., Sisters, Oregon. Copyright © 2000. Used by permission.

"What Does Your Child Need Most?" taken from *What Every Child Needs* by Elisa Morgan and Carol Kuykendall. Copyright © 1997 by MOPS International, Inc. Used by permission of Zondervan Publishing House.

"What Helps You Meet Your Child's Needs?" taken from *What Every Child Needs* by Elisa Morgan and Carol Kuykendall. Copyright © 1997 by MOPS International, Inc. Used by permission of Zondervan Publishing House.

"Encouraging Words" from *The Power of an Encouraging Word* by Ken Sutterfield. Copyright © 1997. Published by New Leaf Press. Used by permission.

"10 Signs of a Great Family" by Dr. Steve Stephens, psychologist and seminar speaker. Copyright © 2001. Used by permission.

"Eight Ways to Practice Humor" by Faith Tibbetts McDonald, writer and editor, condensed from *Christian Parenting Today* magazine, March/April 1999. Used by permission of the author.

"How to Cheer Up Your Children" from *2002 Ways to Cheer Yourself Up* by Cyndi Haynes. Copyright © 1998. Reprinted with permission of Andrews McMeel Publishing. All rights reserved.

"17 Ways to Encourage Reading" from *Ready, Set, Read!* by Barbara Curtis. Copyright © 1998. Published by Broadman & Holman Publishers, Inc., Nashville, Tennessee. Used by permission.

"Benefits When Your Children Enjoy Reading" by Bob Hostetler condensed from *Raising Children by the Books* as published in *HomeLife* magazine, September 2000. Used by permission of the author.

"Great Family Memories" taken from *101 Ideas for Making Family Memories*. Copyright © 2000 by Ruthann Winans and Linda Lee. Published by Harvest House Publishers, Eugene, Oregon 97402. Used by permission.

"10 More Ways to Build a Closer Family" by Dr. Steve Stephens, psychologist and seminar speaker. Copyright © 2001. Used by permission.

"Eight Foundation Builders for Your Family" from *How to Like the Ones You Love* by Susan Alexander Yates. Copyright © 2000. Published by Baker Book House Company, Grand Rapids, Michigan. Used by permission.

"Six Types of Love" taken from *What Every Child Needs* by Elisa Morgan and Carol Kuykendall. Copyright © 1997 by MOPS International, Inc. Used by permission of Zondervan Publishing House.

"10 Essential Toys" by Monica Powers, a creative organizer and mother of three. Copyright © 2001. Used by permission of the author.

"Things to Do with Your Kids" by Harold J. Sala from "Surviving the Summer," *Guidelines for Living* magazine, July/August 2000, pp. 1–2. Used by permission of the author.

"Responsible TV Watching" by Leah Davies condensed from Kelly Bear Web site. www.kellybear.com.

"Pray for Your Children" by John Van Diest, associate publisher. Copyright © 2001. Used by permission of the author.

"Nine Words" from *Life's Little Treasure Book on Marriage and Family* by H. Jackson Brown, Jr. and published by Rutledge Hill Press, Nashville, Tennessee. Used by permission.

"12 Gifts for Your Children" by Dr. Steve Stephens, psychologist and seminar speaker. Copyright © 2001. Used by permission of the author.

"In This Home" by Lisa O. Engelhardt from *In This Home*. Copyright © 1997, Abbey Press, (800) 962-4760. Used by permission.

## WISDOM

"Contrasts for Life" from *Riverside Sermons* by Harry Emerson Fosdick. Copyright © 1958 by Harry Emerson Fosdick, renewed copyright © 1968 by Elinor Fosdick Downs and Dorothy Fosdick. Reprinted by permission of HarperCollins Publishers, Inc.

"Basic Rules" from children ages five to ten, compiled by Dr. Steve Stephens, psychologist and seminar speaker. Copyright © 2001. Used by permission.

"11 Things to Remember" by Ralph Hess, schoolteacher. Ralph Hess practiced typesetting with this list. He exemplified these virtues in over forty years teaching woodshop and over sixty years of perfect Sunday school attendance. He influenced hundred of students through teaching and by example. Used by permission of his widow, Irene Hess.

"Let Us Learn by Paradox" from *The Valley of Vision* by Arthur Bennett. Used by permission of The Banner of Truth.

"Eight Significant Choices" reprinted from *8 Choices That Can Change a Woman's Life*. Revised edition copyright © 1998 by Jill Briscoe. Used by permission of WaterBrook Press, Colorado Springs, Colorado. All rights reserved.

"Take Time" from *Becoming Strong Again* by Gregory L. Jantz. Copyright © 1998. Published by Fleming H. Revell, a division of Baker Book House Company. Used by permission of Gregory L. Jantz, Ph.D., www.aplaceofhope.com.